T0147829

At Full Bloom

Kathleen Wright

iUniverse, Inc.
Bloomington

At Full Bloom

iUniverse books may be ordered through booksellers or by contacting:

iUniverse
1663 Liberty Drive
Bloomington, IN 47403
www.iuniverse.com
1-800-Authors (1-800-288-4677)

Because of the dynamic nature of the Internet, any web addresses or links contained in this book may have changed since publication and may no longer be valid. The views expressed in this work are solely those of the author and do not necessarily reflect the views of the publisher, and the publisher hereby disclaims any responsibility for them.

Any people depicted in stock imagery provided by Thinkstock are models, and such images are being used for illustrative purposes only.

Certain stock imagery © Thinkstock.

ISBN: 978-1-4620-2057-7 (sc)
ISBN: 978-1-4620-2058-4 (e)

Printed in the United States of America

iUniverse rev. date: 06/16/2011

OUTLINE FOR MY MEMOIRS

This is long overdue. In 2008 I watched my 91-year-old father sit with his laptop and resolutely type a synopsis of his life. I was eager for him to do this, because although I was told some of the events in his life, I did not remember and when my children enquired of me and I had forgotten, I went into a self blaming mode and felt guilty because I did what the average human does...I forgot.

These, my memoirs, will be for my children. I currently have no grandchildren and if I do have any in the future and I am too old to remember events and names, then written memoirs will provide them with an idea of my life's activities. I also hope that especially my dear daughter, will gain some insight from this and realize that for me, the bulk of life happened. I lived and I met challenges and dealt with crises as they occurred, mainly through determination, my faith and my gut feeling.

I had to make many decisions in order to move on and continue to live as best as I could at any particular time in my life. Looking back, I have no regrets. I had no instructions, especially on raising children or on spousal roles, except society's and the church's rules ...some of which I broke because as I grew older some were conflicting and created double standards that I was not prepared to live with. This book will appeal to anyone who doubts that God has a sense of humor; or that He is not able to care for people and create resolutions to life's events that the human mind regards as impossible.

In these, my memoirs, two unlikely people (my parents) get married against all odds and with only love and a promise of employment, they remain married for more than six and a half decades. They continue to care for and provide for each other even after the death of one partner.

Two rival siblings (my sister and me), who fought like vixens and constantly competed against each other, become wonderful best friends as adults. They cope with life maturely and as senior citizens, they now can talk about childhood events, compare sexual experiences with honesty and humor that only maturity provides. Two simple, insignificant siblings from a very tiny island, Jamaica, the approximate size of Connecticut USA, evolve through education and a solid, raw, honest upbringing from their parents, manage to succeed against many odds.

A weeping, insecure, naive young girl (me), intolerant of some family members, and condescending favors from some family friends and weary of sexual propositions from 'trusting people', grows to become a professional, a mentor, a lover, a wife and mother, a survivor, a divorcee and a contented senior citizen. This adult learned how to cope with life as it was presented and she learned to watch God unfold in all things and all people daily.

If you the reader sometimes wonder how you will be able to cope or feel that everyone else is coping well, except you…read on and you will discover that many of us have had similar experiences. The difference may be in the time or place of the events and the reality maybe that some of us can talk about events as they happen and some of us, like me, take years to be comfortable enough to share them.

Writing is not easy and I have to be in the mood to do most things. I am sometimes spontaneous and things go very well and sometimes I am the number one procrastinator. My birth sign is Gemini and so that may explain most of my behavior…bipolar to match the two cosmic twins. I became convinced that writing my life story would be a healing process for my entire being and that it may be helpful to my children, who I am sure sometimes need to know about some of my life's experiences…and they may understand me better.

I grew up in a very private long-suffering environment, in which one did not discuss, or consequently appropriately deal with emotional issues. Then it seemed like a good Christian method of suffering through life, because a better life lay ahead, we were taught.

Well, as one gets older certain events start to be contradictory to how one feels and then one begins to shift in deeds and thoughts and decides to live according to what seems right at the time, even if that may be against everything the family grew up to believe at that time. Throughout my life, I have had to change drastically; and I have seen as I age that some of what I thought to be true proved to be the exact opposite and I have felt at ease adjusting to the changes.

An 'Odyssey' can be described as any extended journey.

My life can best be described as a series of odysseys, beginning in Jamaica, a tiny island in the Caribbean Sea, extending to Great Britain and currently settling in the United States of America. For these journeys, my role evolved from that of a frightened youngster, to an independent young adult, an abused wife, a mother, a nurse, a divorcee and now a contented senior citizen in Athens, Georgia. I am also 'at full bloom', remembering all the stages and absolutely enjoying this stage to the best of my ability.

MY FAVORITE YEAR IN SCHOOL

This project is allowing me to look closer at events in my life and to evaluate them briefly, and I guess to find some meaning to why I did some things and what the thought process behind those actions could have been. What was responsible for my actions.

As I got older and gave less thought to what people thought about my actions, and more about how comfortable I felt about some achievements, I acknowledged that people are different and that it is a diverse universe; so I would only drive myself crazy by attempting to please 'all the people all the time'. Now I accept that I am moody and sometimes I am outgoing and accommodating and sometimes I am not. People who know me understand. Those who don't and want to know me better will also understand. The important thing is that I can live with that fact.

Today I look at my school experience and it is difficult to decide which year was best. I really did not enjoy infant/ kindergarten, elementary or high school. Why? I was always in the shadow of my older sister. She was always outgoing, cheerful, easy to talk to, she appeared to be brighter in class and she was stronger than I. This was my perception, and people always expected me to be the same. I, however, was shy. I cried very easily. I was very sensitive and my feelings were easily hurt. I was always ill with any passing virus. I was tall and lanky and the fact that my father fondly called me 'long legs' did not help my self confidence. I did not like most of the children who came to play with us, and I had difficulty mixing with the older children. I must admit that my sister and I fought like vixens…and I did not help because I made it my duty to report every single thing that she did at school that I thought my parents would reward with a quick slap to her rump. The concept of strict discipline preceded child abuse in those days.

Having labored with updating you with my background, my favorite year in school could have been the last year in high school. This was a private high school for girls. My sister had graduated the year before and so finally I felt that I was in charge and independent and got involved in drama and a junior operatic society. I loved singing and meeting peers from the other high schools who were members of this society. We actually performed at one of the local theatres and I enjoyed every moment of that experience. I discovered a new found joy in singing and performing in front of an adult audience. I was intrigued with the make-up artists and fascinated with the transformation of young people to aging adults, just by applying appropriate make-up. I had friends who were going in all directions of life. One pledged to be married and pregnant right after graduation and all I could remember thinking was …*'wow, I could not cope with that change',* I wanted to do more with my life before having children.

I also got closer to some of the girls in my class and at week-ends we would go to the cinema or go to parties at their homes. I had the opportunity to dress up and to really have fun. I enjoyed that period of my life. I loved to dance. I loved the cha-cha-cha and rock-n-roll. My long legs were now shapely and, with nylons and a full skirt made wider with stiff crinolines, I felt that I had an advantage over some of my peers. I also met the brothers of my friends and we just had fun. No dates or romance came from these friendships, it was just understood that a mixed group of us would go together to parties. Of course, the only things my parents allowed their daughters to do were going to parties and to the cinema. Needless to say my father was responsible for our transportation and he made it his duty to find out who the parents of our friends were and ensured that we were collected by midnight.

During my last year in high school, I also had the opportunity to get a holiday job and felt very mature with this accomplishment and got the opportunity to save a few coins independently. It was another source of income beside my allowance. This was only a job at a retail store, but I felt grown up going to work and not school. The owner/manager was very miserly and revealed to me a type of behavior that I knew existed but had not previously seen in adults. The good part of that experience was that there were other students like myself who were also employed for the holiday periods and together we simply laughed at his miserly habits.

At school I had the opportunity to be interviewed by the principal and I discovered that I really admired this woman. I felt that she was actually interested in my welfare and I was thrilled when she added to my recommendation that I had 'a very pleasing personality'. I thought, *'yes… I do agree with you…I do have my own personality'.* I do like people I do like life.

My teachers of English Language and English Literature and Art told me that I showed potential for a career in journalism…I disagreed , I loved

Biology and Botany and thought that I needed to work towards something that utilized Science subjects.

The bottom line is that I was secretly tired of school. I felt that my parents had struggled to pay enough fees for our education and so instead of continuing for another 2 years and then go to college, I opted to leave school at age 16 going on 17 and get a job. This transition was made easier by my paternal uncle giving me the name of the head of personnel at one of the government offices and suggesting that I tell him that I am his niece.

So I left school the Friday, said goodbye to my friends, told my mother that I was not going back and that I was going to work. She did not disagree, but I secretly knew that she could understand how I felt. On Monday I got dressed and visited my uncle's friend and got my first permanent job with the Jamaican government.

MY CHILDHOOD MEMORIES

I must hasten to add that it is not my intention to offend any Jamaican or British National. Some Jamaicans get extremely emotional when discussing politics. These are simply my memories that happened to extend over a period prior to, and after the independence of Jamaica. I am simply trying to recall for my family the effect that some events had on my life.

My parents were both illegitimate (or 'love children' of their parents). Today that would mean nothing, but in the 1940's we were constantly reminded of that fact. My father was born in 1917 and my mother in 1919. My mother's father was also her maternal Aunt's husband and my mother grew up in their home. My maternal grandmother apparently left my mother as a child, migrated to the USA and started a new life there. She also got married and started a new family and, to me, doted over her son and hardly recognized my mom. I will never understand how her mother's sister ever coped with having to raise my mom, but I got the feel of it when my maternal Aunt (her legitimate daughter) refused to acknowledge my sister and me as her relatives.

It must have been difficult for all concerned, but I was more interested in how my mother coped. The interesting thing is that my mother to this day speaks fondly of her father, although sometimes she would say that he was a strict disciplinarian. She also speaks fondly of the home dynamics. I maintain that she has managed to block out all the bitterness of that period and focus on how it should have been. I have grown to forgive my maternal grandmother for her treatment towards my sister and me, especially as she aged and got demented. For a long period of my life I developed a strong feeling of indignation towards anyone from mom's family. I always felt from a very early age that people should forgive and be kind to children.

I realize now that it must have taken intense courage from my maternal grandmother to rise above all that she had to cope with in life and eventually raise her son independently, when, after less than a decade of marriage, she learned that she was married to a bigamist. Today, on December 26ᵗʰ 2010, after talking to my elderly uncle I learned more. He said that my grandmother, his mother, returned to Jamaica with him as a small child when she heard that her mother had cancer. Her marriage dissolved in approximately two years, as she lost contact with her husband. My uncle referred to the loss of contact with his father as, '*his father falling off the map*', two years later. She returned home with her young son and had to live in a family home owned by her sister's husband. It must have been extremely difficult for her.

However, she survived and managed to live independently and work to provide support for herself and her son. Although she would have preferred to ignore my mother, fate had them looking almost like identical twins and on many occasions people whom my mother never knew would approach and address her by her mother's name. This was the beginning of my lessons in life...I later learned that some things that we try to hide eventually surface. I also learned very early that during the process of living, many mental conflicts become evident, making it difficult to follow strict rules about what one will and will not accept, or with whom one will or will not associate.

My father was raised by his mother. She was a very gentle, soft- spoken 'no nonsense' person. I loved her dearly. This lady was a strong supporter of Marcus Garvey and his teaching of African unity and the repatriation of black people to Africa. The interesting thing is that she was a product of Scottish and Jamaican grandparents. She survived two marriages after having dad, and she lived to a grand old age with all her mental faculties intact. She would always tell us folk stories in the Jamaican dialect to make them more intriguing and we always looked forward to seeing and spending time with her.

When my parents got married, my mother's family thought that she could have made a 'better choice' and they always reminded her of it. My father, on the other hand, wanted to marry my mother and pursued her until her father consented. I guess that they were both two obstinate males trying to impress each other.

My parents went to live in the country as a young couple. My father worked as a farm manager and moved from plantation (as they were called) to plantation doing pretty much the same type of job. As children this was wonderful. My sister and I enjoyed it very much. We were big fish in a small pond. My dad was respected in the community and he had a very charming personality. People loved him. My mother was quiet, interested in making home comfortable and keeping her children healthy. She constantly reminded us to 'be careful', and sometimes, looking back, I wonder how we managed to climb trees and go with others into the bushes to play near our home. We lived then in what seemed like large estate houses and enjoyed most of this period of our lives.

The down side to this period was that labor was very volatile. There were times when some people got drunk and threatened my father because they felt that they should be paid more for a specific task. Sometimes issues could be resolved peacefully and sometimes not. My mother always feared pay days as the outcome was unpredictable. I do have memories of one such day having a violent end and we were given police protection to ensure our safety. This lingered forever in my mind and, to this day, I remember thinking as a child how one event could change how some people were perceived. The same group of people who escorted us children to school in the morning…literally saw us as good easy targets in the afternoon. We were bewildered by this behavior but it was an early eye -opener for me.

In addition, my mother extended herself to caring for many people and she would sometimes have to apply tourniquets to bleeding machete wounds, poultices to ulcers and even give subtle family planning advice to women who sometimes asked her.

The machete was the tool of choice for cutting sugar cane, harvesting bananas, chopping open coconuts, digging small holes for planting, weeding, and for clearing land just to name a few uses. It was used for protection and self –defense. It was cheap and readily available. Unfortunately, it was and still is a deadly weapon. In the rural areas it was frequently used to settle disputes, with tragic results. Memories of some incidents still live with me today.

My sister and I attended kindergarten school (or infant school as it was then called) in the country. This was a rural area and what I hated most about the simple school building is that there was no indoor plumbing. I had to use the 'outhouse'. I simply refused, ` accidents' did happen, and then my sister would ignore even knowing me. To this day, if the bathroom is not clean and comfortable, I still have a problem answering 'nature's call'. We changed schools while we were in the country and I do remember the next school was on the first floor of a large building, the upper floor of which was used for Masonic Lodge meetings. Memories here were good.

We moved to the city when I was seven and she was nine. My father lost his job and we came to the city to start a new way of life. I missed the wide open space and the quiet of the country. I missed being able to pick and eat all the different variety of plums and Jamaican apples and an endless supply of ripe bananas and naseberries (a succulent native fruit similar in taste to the persimmon), pineapples, mangoes, and citrus to name a few. The supply was endless. In the city we had to buy everything and the fruits did not seem to be as delicious as those we got in the country.

We were enrolled in an elementary school and my mother had to show our birth certificates to the principal, because she thought that we were older than our age. It did not help when the friend who also accompanied us chirped...

'It is because they have been well fed'.

As time passed though, my family grew very fond of the headmistress and her husband. She also made a lasting impression on our lives. She taught us the importance of our heritage. She taught us about the history of slavery and the slave rebellions on the island. She traced her heritage back to that of a freed slave. We listened in awe, bewildered at the story of slavery, proud of the history of the rebellions and even prouder that this lady could identify family connected to this period.

At this school, we also learned craft. I learned pottery, how to grow plants and make small planters from milk cans, how to care for reptiles... which fortunately, were, turtles. We learned needlework... all these with the basic reading, writing and arithmetic. Schoolchildren kept up to date with politics and current affairs; there was a period on our timetable for listening to the BBC (British Broadcasting Corporation) world news on the radio, and hearing what was happening in the Commonwealth. Jamaica was a British Territory and the colonial governors kept our small island population informed of current events and achievements of the then British Commonwealth.

Me, on the right, with sister,
Thadeen, at approximately age
seven and five, in 1950/51

INTRODUCING MY PARENTS

Growing up there were times when I absolutely disagreed with my parents and their method of parenting. Sometimes, looking back, it was when we were teenagers, my sister and I would meet up with our friends and we would complain bitterly. To us it was a good time to compare notes on how we were parented and the difficult things that we were experiencing. We complained that our parents were too strict. We were not allowed to buy all the popular records that we liked. Some, they said, were vulgar, and had no meaning… Bill Haley, Elvis Presley, two of the many famous names that immediately come to mind…they 'gyrated' and young men should not behave like that. The lyrics had no meaning and they were too repetitive.

'There was nothing to be learned from those pop songs' ,my mother would say.

We could read some comic books but the popular 'all in pictures', the small love story comics, were out of bounds. One day my father caught me engrossed and completely absorbed, eagerly reading an 'all in picture' story… he had not seen them before. He borrowed it to read for himself, and, as my luck would have it, he thought that it was not appropriate reading material. We continued to keep up to date with these by hiding the books and reading when we could, in secret. Also 'unfair' was that the movies that we were allowed to see at the cinema were censored. Life was unfair and we girls were not happy. Male company was approved only if our parents knew the young men's parents. We attended a private high school for girls and so we could not pass off new male company as 'boys from school'.

Looking back though, as frustrating as it was, they (my parents) must have done something right, or they may have scared us into following most of their rules…because although we thought at the time that we were rebellious, we were angels compared to some trouble that other children got involved in.

I also believe that my sister fared better than I did because she enjoyed wonderful relationships and she did not get married, and she did not have any children. I remind her that she is lucky when sometimes she wonders if she would have been able to cope as a mother. She did not have to contend with a partner's mid life crisis and she does not have to answer the 'mom why did you and what were you thinking of when you...' questions that my children ask. I find myself answering...'I had no instruction manual, it seemed to be the right thing to do at that time'.

I also know that our parents did a good job, when I went to nursing school. I was miles away from home in a foreign environment. At first, I hated it, and there were times when I wondered if I had made the wrong decision. On each occasion, I decided to face my problems and continue, and the longer I remained the more I discovered that almost everyone felt the same. The truth is that I respected my parents very much and as much as I did have bad days, I did not consider giving up and returning home. That will -power I owe to them.

To those of us who believe in predestination, some will say, that my birth was already planned by the Divine power. I can only say as a simple human being, that if it were not for my parents I would never have been born. Consequently, although I am no millionaire, or super human, I had no hesitation in inviting them to spend their last days in my home. I would be naïve to say that it has been easy. There were times that I cringed when I saw my dad balance his 180+ lb frame sitting with my frail chair turned backwards. I thanked God that he was OK when I realized that he stubbornly sat and resolutely planted half the number of crepe myrtle trees while I was away, because he knew that I intended doing it alone. I watched a tall, husky, stern disciplinarian turn into a supporting, understanding person with whom I could talk plainly about anything. He also cried easily when he was elderly, he would cry as he hugged his grandchildren when he saw them; or when he spoke of his childhood and the role that his mother played in coping as a single mother, in the rough days of his upbringing. He admitted to me that he cried when he saw me leave home to go to work in the snow while my husband stayed behind. I remember his asking me with tears in his eyes...

'What have you taken on to yourself Ms. Margaret? Your mother's memory is gone and I move at snail's pace', then I reassured him with wet eyes that together we would be able to cope.

I truly loved my father and remember him fondly but never with sadness. He had a dry wit, he had a sweet charm and the ladies adored him...much to my mother's annoyance. He loved my mother, although when I was younger I did not think so. One day he said to me:

'Today is our 68th anniversary'...I knew that he was not senile and I also knew that they were only married for 66 years…so he waited for me to ask the obvious question and then he replied with a twisted smile:

'Today is 68 years since our first date'.

To this day, each time I arrange for a sitter to remain with my mother; I thank God that my father had the foresight to prepare for these days. He got frailer in the final days of his chronic illness and I prayed that he would keep his dignity to the end and my prayers were answered. The night before he died, he fell as he stubbornly tried to get to the bathroom independently. I remember praying that we would all be able to cope with his final moment. He slept that night. The next morning he allowed me to assist him with a bed bath. I applied Shea butter to his back and to the dry skin of his legs and feet. The day before he also allowed me to shave him and trim his hair and he looked in the mirror afterwards and commented…

'You may be able to do this for a living'.

The morning of his death he tidied himself, had a cup of coffee agreed that he really felt comfortable, that he was pain free; he looked at his wristwatch and suggested that I should leave him 'for a little while,' as Jamaicans say. I left the room to check on my mother who was getting out of bed to have her breakfast. As I carried her tray into her room I glanced at my father, out of habit, his head hung backwards, awkwardly. Instinctively, I realized that he was dead.

It was my first experience with death involving the immediate family. I remembered that he did not want to be resuscitated, and, as I called 911, I remember saying…

'I am not even sure whom to call'.

They responded by sending the Emergency Medical Team and they confirmed that he was dead. The Coroner came and these folks were very professional. They comforted us and they even called a neighbor to sit with us because they did not feel comfortable leaving my mother and me alone. I accepted that my father was dead and I felt very empty.

The family had worked well in preparing for this moment and as soon as my sister, my children and my newly found brother came to us, together we followed my father's plans for the final disposition of his body. We did this as a united family, thanks to our father. His body was cremated; his service was a cheerful family re-union looking back at his life as someone who understood well how to live and how to cope with aging and how to accept things what he could not change, and to work ceaselessly at changing what he could.

I will always miss him, I will always think fondly of him as his memory lingers in my heart. My first experience with the death of a parent can be summarized as …a wonderful life story in which I had a role. I can look back with satisfaction and say…

'Thank you dad, you gave me life. I am so grateful to God that I was able to direct my love and care and career skills to making life and your final days comfortable and stress free'.

Seated in front is my mother's grandmother(Catherine Powell), on left is my mother's brother(Douglas Grant), and on the right is my mother's first cousin, Joy Jones Heron

JUST WORKING WAS NOT WORKING FOR ME

Well, I was adamant on my decision to leave school. I had been working for about two years before I decided that I wanted to do something more with my life. This could have been my first attempt to periodically review my life and accomplishments and then make decisions on my future and plans for coping, and for social and psychological survival. There were many factors that led me to leave Jamaica in the 1960's. As I write these notes I will also include a quotation that I recently heard, it was …'if you want God to laugh, tell Him your plans for the future'.

On the surface, my life seemed to be going all right. I had some friends, some of whom I kept in touch with from school and some I met through work. I was also dating a very charming young man who was the son of the minister of my church. This was a new role for me. I must admit that I am an incurable romantic and, at that stage of my life, I was very young, naïve, shy in the company of males, awe struck and vulnerable. I cannot say what I was looking for in a partner, except someone who was honest and who had goals for self development that were similar to mine. He had a wonderful tenor voice and he would sing at church concerts and functions. I was bewitched especially when he sang Nat King Cole's "Stay as sweet as you are" in my ear. I repeat…I was awe struck. He, (I will call my friend Burns), did share with me that he wanted to be a minister like his father. I must have assumed at that time that our relationship was leading to marriage.

In a sense I was happy to be dating this young man or happy just to be dating. I felt so secure when we went to the cinema and he would hold my hand against his face, or gently kiss my hand. However, then I was a shy, subdued individual and there were issues that I took for granted. I assumed that if I were in love, then my friend (Burns) would also be in love with me, especially as we were kissing and holding hands whenever we were together. First, I had to get used to my new romantic role with this handsome young man who was everyone's favorite and my very first love. The down side to this friendship was that his was a troubled family. His mother had a strong, controlling personality that I found intimidating.

Silently, I was not happy with the overall current *status quo* of my life. That *status quo* included routinely getting up and going to work, leaving work and going to extra classes, going to the movies in my spare time and going to church with my parents. I knew that there was more to life and I wanted to find it. If I continued in this mode, I could see that I would eventually be married and then I felt it would be too late to do whatever else I may discover that I could do. Some of my friends were married, and they seemed to be happy, but in my eyes, they seemed to be almost totally dependent on their husbands. What about their personal plans for self development? Did they just get shelved after marriage? That is how it appeared to me. Then came their children and the beginning of an entirely new chapter started in their life, their role as parents. I was ready for romance, but not for an early marriage and I was not ready to have children before I had the opportunity to travel. My love affair ended when my friend migrated. He was off to begin college in order to fulfill his dream to become a minister of religion.

After leaving home, he never wrote to me. I was surprised and upset and I really could not talk openly about this to anyone…because I was also embarrassed. I did not feel that anyone could understand the extent of my sadness and that if I shared my feelings, I would probably be told that it was only 'puppy love'. Now more than ever, I wanted to broaden my horizons.

My mother was a stay at home mom. She had her own demons in life that she had to cope with. She regularly preached to us the importance of a good education and she always said…

'Do not just get a job. Get a career…before you get married'.

She urged my sister and me never to be dependent on a husband to provide for us. I am sure she had some regrets of her own, regarding her marriage, but she accepted the role of a dutiful wife and mother and she lives that role still today. She spent many, too many, sad moments crying and moping, and doubting the sincerity of some of the family's friends. She also was not a good social mixer and in a way I can empathize. However, if we, my sister and I, lived by those rules, we never would have left home and seen for ourselves what life was like elsewhere beyond that tiny land mass in the Caribbean Sea.

I also realized very early that my meager salary was not enough to make travel possible. Nor would I be able to live independently, if I decided to remain in Jamaica. I had never traveled away from home, but deep within my soul, I yearned to do so. I watched the Commonwealth news as it was shown on the cinema screens prior to any movie and I was fascinated with news on countries of the British Commonwealth and I would listen to foreign delegates' speeches at international conferences and constantly learned about current events from countries in the Caribbean, Africa, Gibraltar, South America, the United Kingdom and others. I was ready to explore beyond my comfort zone, and to meet more people, to experience other cultures and learn more. I felt trapped, encased in the culture of my tiny island but unable to physically and emotionally experience any other. Now I must explain that there were other nationalities residing in Jamaica, but I learned their culture second hand, I wanted to experience it.

My job was not threatened, but it was boring. I kept it because it was the thing to do. I also felt some loyalty to my uncle who was instrumental in getting me employed and I feared that he would think that I was ungrateful if I resigned. Then, my work involved going to the Tax Revenue offices and editing the 'books of receipts' to ensure that the entries of the previous day's transactions were appropriate. There were obviously no computers and the books were heavy and dusty. It was a boring routine that I did not find challenging.

My sister left home for England in 1964 to go to nursing school. Now to me, prior to leaving Jamaica, she seemed to have been doing well. She certainly earned more than I did and her job on leaving school was certainly more glamorous and mentally stimulating than mine. Although she did not share her deep reasons with me until many years afterwards. She stated that she also had arrived at a cross roads in her life. She accepted traveling overseas as her escape.

England seemed then to be the natural country of choice, as it was the country of our former colonizers. It was also easier, we thought, to acquire an Entry Permit from the British High Commissioner than to commence the tedious task of endless paperwork necessary to acquire a visa to travel to the United States. We felt that the culture would be familiar. Because one was given free room and board, and a stipend during training, acceptance to a British school gave us the opportunity to travel, study and receive some money during the period of training. It was our answer to changing our *status quo*. We also decided that a career in healthcare would guarantee job security.

Neither of us knew what nursing training entailed. We had previously visited people in the hospital when they were ill, but to understand what it meant to be working in that setting was absolutely as foreign as going to England. We heard of many people who had gone there before we did, but we never kept in touch to hear exactly how they coped. Looking back, my sister never really gave any 'pointers' explaining what the transition was like for her. Remembering our relationship though, that was not strange.

So following in my sister's footsteps, I applied to and was accepted by the Guildford School of Nursing and left Jamaica in April 1966. It was very difficult to leave my mother. She was now older, and with my sister gone, mom probably thought that I would have remained at home. My father remained and worked in the country and he would return to our home in the city every fortnight. It would mean that with me leaving, my mother would be alone. Although she did not ask me to stay with her, she probably prayed that I would. I loved my mother and it was a very difficult decision to leave. On the other hand, this was about my future and I wanted to grab the opportunity to try something new and create a plan for my personal growth.

I traveled via the United States and divided my 10 day stay in New York between my mother's brother and an old Aunt. On arrival they both made every effort to impress me with what they knew of the city. I was shown the flashing neon lights, the fast food shops, the supermarkets, and large department stores. Those folks were so busy working that they had no time to explore and to learn about their new home; I realize now that they were merely trying to survive. I asked to go to the Planetarium and I found it strange that they had to ask for directions, and that they were visiting this place for the very first time. If I wanted to go for a walk, I was told how dangerous it was and that it was too cold and that I would get ill. My uncle's wife also seemed to be surprised that I could not cook. I was meeting her for the first time and I did not have an opportunity to know and to understand her personality. She probably thought that I was going to prepare all the meals during my visit. I felt that I was being treated like a child and I was overjoyed when those ten days passed and I left the USA for London. I did not enjoy my initial visit to the United States. Little did I know what God had in store for me.

My flight over was 8 hours long…I arrived in May decked out in a black winter coat with a fur collar, compliments of my elderly Aunt, who meant well. It was a warm coat, but unfashionable and I did not have the heart or courage to hurt her feelings, so I wore it. I arrived at London's Heathrow airport early in the morning and there waiting for me was my dear older sister. Her face was a welcome sight and of course, she was the only person whom I knew in this part of the world. We embraced, and we were like two solitary souls, bonded by sisterhood and ready to stick with each other, 'through thick and thin'. We had dared to step out of the comfort zone of a very sheltered upbringing and to embark on the unfamiliar path that lay ahead of us. My sister continues on that path even today.

It was grey and cold and misty…people had a fixed smile on their faces, but their eyes did not reflect warmth. We traveled by bus to the Methodist

International House in London's West End. I would stay there for a week to get acclimatized to Britain and London before going to Guildford in the country. My sister stayed with me for two days and she would return and accompany me to Guildford. Our British born, Methodist Minister in Jamaica, recommended this hostel to us. It would prove to be a welcome escape during my holidays from training. At the hostel we shared room with 4 other ladies, who were from other Caribbean islands. We became friends almost immediately and they all, including my sister, started to 'brief' me on nuances of British behavior and the initial scrutinizing that I would experience from my adopted hosts, and most importantly, that I would have to keep focused on my goals in order to accomplish them.

ENGLAND, THE MOTHER COUNTRY

Writing this is extremely difficult and it has brought to the forefront memories that I tried hard to live through and tried hard to forget. Although we all prove over time, that, although we live through difficult times, the memory lingers forever.

It was my decision to go to England. I did not know the details of what learning nursing involved, but I wanted to learn. Traveling to England showed me another aspect of human behavior. It showed me a world that thought I did not possess the ability to be successful. This world assumed that I lived under primitive, substandard conditions; it assumed that I should accept without question what I was told and that I should be grateful for what England had done for my fellow citizens. Some people with whom I came in contact were rude and insulting and told me in outspoken terms that I was not welcome. This world seemed to assume that I had no emotion, that I was immune to insults and, at five foot and ten inches, that I was invisible.

I learned to fight back with words. I learned to correct misconceptions of my heritage and my culture with eloquence. I slowly gained acceptance and respect by demanding respect as an intelligent human being.

I was so homesick that I could have easily been physically ill. During the first three months in England, I gained weight rapidly. The diet was different, with more carbohydrates. It was enticing, with mid morning coffee and afternoon tea breaks. There were confectionary shops with unique displays of chocolates and candy. The corner shop bakeries with wonderful freshly baked loaves, coupled with my feeling of independence and being miles away from home, did not help. Soon the scales tipped well over on the other side to my disadvantage and several dress sizes larger.

It was challenging working on the children's ward. I had to quickly ditch my Jamaican accent in order that the children would be able to understand me. It was difficult to cope with a ward full of sick and dying children. The harshness of this adventure was that it gave me no time to stop and fret on homesickness. When I yearned to see the familiar faces of my parents and family, I would re-focus on my ultimate goal and simply pray for courage to be successful. What also helped me to remain focused on my goals was a wonderful informal support group of fellow students, of all ages, from the Caribbean. I listened to their experiences and their hints on coping. We bonded well, and, with the help of this group I managed to identify characters on faculty, who were vindictive, insulting and downright evil. I was forewarned and so fortunately, I was able to anticipate the 'obstacles' placed on my course. I also decided that if others with more disadvantages than me could be successful, there was no reason why I could not do the same.

'You need to focus and study and pass that exam at the end of the first three months, because if you fail, you will not be allowed to continue and you will have to return home', they said sternly.

Now this was never explained in any brochure or correspondence, and I welcomed the tip because during this period there were many distractions. I was always enticed to go places and sometimes I felt that I was enticed to stay out late. My mentors forewarned me of this. They reminded me that I could stay out as long as I liked, but at the end of that day I had to include study time, because there were no exceptions to the rules; if I failed I would be sent home.

'You are going to see that you are the only candidate from overseas in your group'.

They were correct, I was the lone one from overseas, the 'foreigner'. I was also advised by my 'Home Sister' (the nurse who was similar to a 'House Mother')...

'Do not blame everything that you are told on the fact that you are black dear'. (Everything good or bad, always ended with this word of endearment... 'dear'); and there was always reference to the weather, when I said,

'Good morning', people asked ...

'What is good about it?'

Some of my fellow students did reach out to me and invited me to their homes on some weekends and I welcomed this. I soon discovered that some homes in the country did not have full indoor plumbing, and that 'out houses' still existed. All washing, I noticed was done at the kitchen sink. There was a towel rack for the kitchen towels and another for the bath towels. This was eye opening for me, because England was 'the Mother Country'. On a more personal note, I sent samples of the toilet paper from public facilities, home as evidence; it bore a strong resemblance to parchment paper. It was stiff and unrelenting.

God places His people on earth to remind others that the entire world is not evil. So I can say that I also met some very kind people. I did get invited to a fellow student's home one weekend and so I had a glimpse of the intact family unit and feel hospitality. There was also an unforgettable older nurse who 'mothered' my sister and me and that friendship continued until her death, long after I returned to Jamaica. I also met my best friend Jane during this era and we had a wonderful friendship and great fun together. She got married before we graduated and she had three sons. She went to live in Belgium. Sadly her marriage fell apart and as the years passed we lost contact with each other. I think about her constantly.

My sister remained in England and made it her home. Over the last forty six years she has a wonderful network of friends who can be regarded as family. They are now our extended family. The Atlantic Ocean physically separates us but we all keep in contact with each other through the years exchanging info now on grandchildren, as different eras of our lives unfold with time.

Today, as I spoke with my sister, she reminded me that it was forty-six years to the day since she left Jamaica for England.

'What have I really done in that time?' she asked skeptically. 'I have nothing to show'.

We had a 'Now just you look here moment', time in which I carefully itemized what she had in fact accomplished:-

She was the silver medalist (Salutatorian) in her group of nursing students.

She left the National Health employment and moved into the private sector, eventually co-owning a rest home, which she later sold for a handsome profit.

She bought and completely paid for her home.

She owned rental property and walked away from it with no losses.

She stepped away from nursing with no physical or legal injuries.

She has been able to enjoy her retirement and enjoy her life's milestones.

She was able to visit our parents frequently and stay with them for longer periods as they aged.

It is amazing how quickly the years go by. My sister saw England as her new home. On the other hand, I kept in touch with my friends at home and eventually returned home to nurse my own people. Then I was fiercely patriotic. Jamaica was a new nation and I wanted to return to be a part of that era. Continuing my nursing career there seemed like a practical route to take. I had also met my future husband who still resided on the island, and I felt that I was ready for marriage and a family of my own.

Traveling to England enabled me to fulfill my career dreams. It also gave me a crash course on reality and on growing up. Many of the bitter experiences were very hard to cope with. I emerged with a career and a strong spirit of determination to meet and view life as it is. I learned to honestly admit my shortcomings and recognize how to correct some, and to be comfortable with those that I choose not to correct. I have also learned that hardly any of society's rules are etched in stone. I emerged never doubting myself and never for a split second classifying myself as second class to any of the world's citizens. I passionately accept that if anyone is given a fair, honest and unbiased education and is allowed fair access to society's resources, the world can be anyone's oyster.

Two and a half decades later, this experience made me decide that my young children needed to experience the opportunity of graduating from an educational system that was globally recognized. Looking back, I subconsciously pledged that I owed it to my offspring to pave their road to social mobility.

My sister, as a young student nurse in Guildford, Surrey, England, 1964　　*Me, as a young student nurse in Guildford, 1966*

THE DAY I BECAME ONE OF THEM!

This event happened while I was doing my midwifery training in Surrey, England. I was young and loving life. Parties were frequent and I was always present. I loved good company, good drinks and dancing. I flirted easily and enjoyed all for the hell of it. Of course, I was at least 20 pounds lighter in body weight, I kept my hair straightened and at shoulder length. It was a lovely spring morning and I had two hours off before returning for the remainder of my shift. The sun was unusually bright in exceptionally blue skies. I have to emphasize the beauty of the day, because, looking back, these days were not frequent.

I decided to go into the town and walk around aimlessly, probably have a cup of coffee at the Wimpy shop. I had to walk away from the training scenario for a few hours. There would be no monitors, no crying babies, no monitoring of dilating cervices, no glaring looks from my thyrotoxic clinical instructor, who kept turning off the heat, because she was always too hot.

I had recently acquired a Gina Lolobrigida wig. It was brown. My hair was jet black, and short, my hair was long. I thought…`just what I needed, something different`. I was wearing this wig for the first time. So off to town I went, starting at the bus stop. I had on a green, double breasted mini coat with gold buttons, knee high black boots, black leather gloves and I felt good… the wig made me look different.

Well, the bus stop was some distance away, on the straight road ahead of me. As I walked I could see the bus approaching, and if I missed it I would have to wait another hour. This was in the country…an hourly interval was good. `Well`, I thought quickly, `a good sprint would be not be difficult`, so I decided to run for the bus. I already knew that the driver would not be stopping to pick me up away from the designated stop. The rules had to be adhered to by the letter.

I sprinted easily and made it to the bus stop on time. I got on board.

'Oh'…the older women were all saying loudly…

'She must be an athlete, oh my, she sprinted so well…and looked so good'.

My ego continued to soar, and I walked to the front of the bus and sat in the only remaining seat behind the driver. From this seat one could look into the driver's large rear view mirror…and, being young and vain, I looked into it. My Gina's wig was at an angle that could only be described as treacherously crooked. It hung haphazardly on my right ear…exposing my black hair that was below and, needless to say, the fringe was at a miserable angle! There was nothing glamorous or fashionable with this image, and I was sitting at the front of the wretched bus!

I had to regain control of the situation, I looked directly into the mirror, decided quickly that I had to correct the angle and did so with dignity and grace and continued to stare straight ahead of me. God bless those women. Nobody laughed, nobody smiled, nobody reacted at all and I walked from that bus with the elegance of royalty, praying that none of those passengers would ever see me again!

My ego was whipped, but I cheered myself up by thinking realistically well, at home there is an old saying that most of the British are crazy, so here probably they also feel that most of us blacks, especially from the Caribbean, are crazy also…today they saw it in living color.

MY RETURN HOME

I still had this patriotic urge to return home to nurse my fellow compatriots. I had no idea what nursing in Jamaica was like prior to leaving nor did I know what it would be like, now that I was back, but here I was and I was ready to face the challenge. Socialized medicine existed in Jamaica, in theory. The main parishes, of which there were fourteen, all seemed to have hospitals. To work in any of these hospitals, one applied through the Ministry of Health. There was the risk that the applicant could be sent anywhere island wide, where there was the need for nurses. Of course getting into a hospital near home seemed to depend on who the applicant was and how well one was known. The patients were hardworking people in society who desperately needed help.

The 'private hospitals' were less crowded and served a population that could pay for services, through private insurance provided from their employment contract. Or they were mostly 'business people' who had no hardship in paying for their health care expenses. I applied for and got a job at a private hospital, run by the Catholic Church. I worked here as a midwife. My skills were hardly utilized as deliveries were controlled by private doctors who charged fees for their services to oversee the natural process of childbirth. Sometimes they miscalculated and missed the birth, and, on those rare occasions, I had the thrill of being a part of that beautiful process of natural childbirth, from the patient's admission to the birth of her baby. Interestingly enough, the majority of patients and their significant others felt that a midwife was an encumbrance and saw no reason for their presence as a part of the delivery team. Patient education here was prejudiced against a group of efficient professionals in favor of another selfish group that was not at all willing to work with anyone else, even if, in the long term, it would be to the advantage of all who were involved.

I have strong feelings on this subject and feel that Obstetricians are necessary to follow complicated pregnancies that may inevitably end in difficult deliveries. However, a healthy pregnant adult who carries a baby to term can use the services of a midwife, at home or in the hospital. I still take that stand today, three decades plus later, when it is being revealed that many Cesarean Sections and labor inductions are unnecessary, and place the expectant mother at unnecessary health risks.

It was however, my choice to work at this hospital and so I stayed there. Interestingly enough, I also discovered that somehow I was alienated by some at work and by some in society. Many referred to me as 'one of those who ran away when things were rough'. Sometimes it was felt that I thought that I was better than others were because I went to England. Although I lived in Jamaica many more years than I was absent doing nursing, some people felt that they had to explain basic things peculiar to the Jamaican society...I constantly had to remind my compatriots that I knew all about my homeland. I felt that I could do better working elsewhere, and that I needed to work in a teaching hospital environment. There I could also continue my career growth. I also thought that since I would be married by the end of the year, I would delay changing jobs until afterwards. Going back home to occupy my old room and to live with my parents was interesting. Sometimes I was treated as an adult, but sometimes in making decisions for myself, I felt that I was not in control, regardless of how much I spoke out. I still was not earning enough to live independently. My salary was $30.00 a week...the harsh truth of Third World progress.

My love life was going well. I loved the fact that I had a friend in my ex-husband. The friendship provided a psychological escape from the reality of home life and work issues. We seemed to talk easily about trivial things. I did not see how he reacted around children. I discovered that he had many siblings, about ten, and many of his older siblings were sisters. They seemed to have replaced the role of their mother who was deceased, and he never said 'no' to anything they asked of him. I seemed to have been cautiously scrutinized by them and so I really never felt that I would ever be a part of their group. My stubborn nature responded by being indignantly self-assured that I was involved with their brother and not them.

Well, soon our love child was on the way. I was pregnant, much to my father's disappointment.

'You are a nurse and should have been more careful' he told me. My mother cried, but said that we were adults and she would support me in my new role. The December wedding date was brought forward to October. My father still offered to pay for the reception, but he constantly reminded me that I could have done better with my life. Secretly I discovered many years later that he did not like my choice. He felt that my now, ex- husband was very conceited and too defensive on too many topics, feeling that his opinion was the only one that was significant.

We got married. Some family friends were extremely vocal in expressing their disappointment on my pregnancy. I responded by mentally noting whom I regarded as true friends. We lived in the small half of a two family house… we were in the same city as my parents and most of my new husband's siblings. Everyone was about five to ten miles away.

My new role as a mother was very challenging. I knew theoretically about most of these events but personally experiencing them was enlightening. I experienced physiological body changes after childbirth, I learnt to cope with post partum blues, I learnt to comfort my colicky baby, or my baby who did not want to sleep when his parents were tired. I learnt to soothe tender gums during his teething experience. All these events I taught mothers repeatedly. Now it was personal and exhaustingly beautiful. My husband seemed very proud that he was the father of a son. He did help …we coped. We enjoyed our family capsule. Here we made and changed the rules. Things were going well.

WORKING WIFE AND MOTHER

We can all claim to see clearly in hindsight and I am no exception. Looking back, I can recall events that could be noted as warning signs and they went unheeded. Sometimes I suppose that I overlooked these signs, because I tried to think that I was coping with minor human faults. I also felt that I had already decided to get married and so I never thought of canceling the wedding. I focused on a wedding and not on marriage. My dress was almost finished. My father agreed to pay for the wedding reception at a local hotel, and reservations were already made. The church was already booked for the wedding ceremony, and I never thought of canceling my wedding. When I noticed new behavioral changes in my future husband, I chose to call them 'trivial' and continued with wedding plans. I thought that I was mature to make my decisions, but clearly, I was not. I also had my own ideas about love and marriage and I wanted my experience to be nothing like that of my parents. I watched my mother cry a lot during her marriage and sometimes she seemed to accept as destiny the role of 'the suffering wife'. Ironically, I walked into her shoes in that role…as much as I thought that I would steer clear of it.

Being totally honest to this union, I told my husband of relationships that I had prior to dating him. I thought that I would be honest and share this part of my life with him. I also thought that most of this happened while I was in England and I did not want him to hear anything through a third party. He, in return, told me of the wonderful women whom he dated and what he missed about them. He also threw what I can describe as a "temper tantrum" when he heard my news, and informed me, "that type of behavior would not be tolerated by him". All I did was to tell him about the single men whom I had dated. Now I think that he over-reacted, but then I dismissed it by reassuring myself that I had no future cause for concern, because I did not intend on having affairs while I was married and so a repetition of this behavior from him would be unlikely.

Another warning sign was that he was supposed to find us somewhere to live when I returned from England. He failed to do this. I also found out that he opted to live as a lodger with families, and so he had no idea of the cost of food, utilities and basic expenses. He also changed addresses very frequently, as he suspected that 'people were searching his belongings' in his absence. Again I took no notice. After we were married he displayed bizarre signs of jealousy and was suspicious of my older male family friends, my colleagues, anyone. This man was nine years my senior and I thought that was to my advantage.

As a family, first, we resided near to my family, and, as time passed, we moved further away from everyone. Finally, our last home prior to migrating was an old split level structure miles away from and above the city. It was located on a steep incline surrounded by multiple fruit trees with few, equally isolated, neighbors. For the first time in my life, we were victims of a burglary that, fortunately, occurred while we were away from our home. I lived in fear for our lives as violence escalated and my husband seemed to see it as a lovely place for the children to play in the country. A very outspoken colleague said jokingly:

"Your husband always seems to be hiding his family and this time he has succeeded".

For many years I never told my parents the problems that I was having with my marriage, neither did I share my thoughts on his stormy, jealous outbursts. I hated to hear the words *I told you so*.

Our son was a lovely child. He loved his father and looked up to him. Somehow, my husband appeared to have difficulty bonding with him as he grew older. While he was an infant, my husband was a very patient father. He would sit up at nights literally rocking our son to sleep. He would also feed him sometimes to allow me to rest. As our son grew older, however, my husband felt that boys should be hardy and not pampered. Although he was a sports fanatic, I do not remember his playing any sport with his son or teaching him any sport. I do not remember them doing anything special together. Recently, however, my son reminded me that he remembered his dad making him a kite and showing him how to fly it.

Our child started school at age four. That was the norm. Private Preparatory Schools accepted their students at that age. He could read, write some script, spell his name, and we both thought he was ready for an introduction to teaching in a playschool setting. At age six my husband insisted that our son could take the bus home, on the days that he, my ex, had to travel out of town. I could not drive and I felt that I was not in control, and I went along with this decision. During this period I had no one with whom I could share my marital problems. We were controlled with an iron fist and I allowed it to continue. I went along with this decision until finally we all agreed that since school was nearer to my parents' home, our son could go there after school and then we would all ride home together when I left work.

Prior to starting Prep School, my son bonded well with his grandparents. They were inseparable and they provided a stable family unit on which he thrived. After school, their home provided a retreat for us to relax. He could play as a child and I could feel uninhibited to enjoy a break from a psychological bonding force that I felt kept me in this marriage.

MY ROLE: WORKING MOTHER, WIFE, NURSE

Writing about this period of my life is extremely difficult. Some events, as I remember them, reflect an eerie picture that I prolonged a process that caused pain and suffering for my children and that it could have been avoided. I felt a strong bond with my church and my Christian upbringing, but it was not until very late in my marriage that I felt that I was pretending. To everyone else and on Sundays, I pretended that we were a loving family. During the week, there was no pretense and the regular quarrels and shouting matches continued. When I finally realized this pretense, I opened my thoughts to the subject of divorce and convinced myself that it was the 'healthy' choice to make.

I did this to my children. What was I thinking? I can only hope that they will not make this same mistake and also that they will be able to forgive me for exposing them to that aspect of behavior. The role the church instilled in me was that I felt it was normal to suffer in life. I also felt that marriage was for a lifetime and if you made the wrong choice…that somehow…you (both spouses) could work through problems. To do that, however, it takes two people talking through issues, forgiving each other, and compromising each other's goals for one better goal that would be best for the family. There is no room for selfishness. In my opinion, I was always blamed for failures. I never seemed to be able to say the right thing to my then husband. I always yearned to hear 'I love you' or 'I really am sorry'. Those words never came in the context that I wanted to hear. I was a 'die hard' romantic and so I stayed married.

We had another child. She was a beautiful baby girl. As she grew, she met all her developmental milestones early, she adored her father and she loved her big brother. She was bossy and spoke her mind. As a young lady she gives all her love, and she is a beautiful person inside and out. Both of our children have matured into wonderful adults. They are both very caring people, both are goal oriented and both are very well in tune with how the world functions.

After writing these memoirs, I may have to write about my nursing career in more detail, because the three aspects of my life were profound. Marriage, motherhood and career growth were all occurring at the same time. Marriage was emotionally destructive (although it took many years to come to that conclusion). Work was essential to keep us financially intact and nursing provided ongoing career challenges that helped me to mature, and to accomplish career goals that I never thought were possible.

My emotional pain deepened when I experienced my first incident of physical abuse. Here I was, the nurse in charge of a unit, a team leader and an administrator. It was the end of a very busy year. An annual meeting was scheduled and it was decided that after the meeting we, the staff, would have a social. At this time all our patients and their potential issues were plotted and a projected plan was identified for each individual. It was crucial that I attend. My husband insisted that anything arranged after 4 pm was not work related and that I should not attend. I disagreed. I arranged for my mother to come to our home and baby-sit the children, and I arranged a drive from a colleague, who also said that he did not plan staying at the social for a long time, and that I could travel with him.

The meeting went well, and my home was intact, but my husband was sulking. A few days later, my husband and I were talking. During all this, I held my infant daughter on my hip I had no idea how angry he was, and as I turned around to face him, I felt the full force of his fist on my face. I was punched in my face by this man, as I held our child. He angrily said…

'Now you get to work and show your man what I thought about your little meeting'.

I was distraught, I felt my world shatter…how could he do this? How could he even think like that? I cried and I stayed home until my face was healed and I stayed away from explaining anything to my parents. I told my elderly paternal grandmother, who wept and said…

'In my life I was hit once and after I returned it …he never went that route again'.

I did not want to be fighting anyone I also knew that I could not physically fight any male, I could not compete with Testosterone and muscle. When he returned home that evening and went to bed, I said to him in a very quiet voice …

'I know that I cannot fight you. I am not strong enough. I also know that I am not going to have this incident repeated, so here is the plan. I have not acted crazy before, but if you ever hit me again you will always remember that you are married to and that you hit a crazy woman'.

'What do you think you can do?' he chuckled…

'Try testing me whenever you are ready', I said quietly,' I may not win physically, but you will never forget that day.' I promised.

It took another two decades before a repeat performance occurred, and I was so startled at my angry response that I confirmed …it was time to quit this union.

RAISING OUR CHILDREN

There were many times when we literally survived daily. We could not do long term planning. Many of our friends at home and at work were leaving Jamaica to seek employment elsewhere. The cost of living was increasing at a frightening rate. Our goals were repeatedly shoved forward by many years. It was frustrating to plan ahead because one never seemed to be in full control of one's life. Many other variables shattered dreams in our Third World environment. When the price of oil increased internationally, our country had no money to meet this increase, so taxes were increased. The local currency that already was non -competitive on the international market was devalued, increasing the cost of living expenses for the island's citizens. Industrial disputes were frequent and so were workers' strikes. People, working people, like us, felt as if we were squeezed to the core and our survival was threatened. Crime increased, and for me, going to work in the depressed area of the city always proved to be challenging. To encourage staff retention, members of our hospital got a small stipend just for working there. We referred to it as 'danger pay'.

Nurses also went on strike for more pay, and for better working conditions, and, because of this, we were targeted as being unsympathetic to the government. At home we economized to the best of our ability and we still had to struggle. Life, of course, continued and we had a family to support. I tried to leave nursing, intending to work in another government ministry (department), hopefully for a higher salary. I was blocked because I was told that I was one of the few nurses who knew dialysis and therefore it was crucial for me to stay. On the other hand, I could not get any extra money, because there was none. I enjoyed my work, but I felt as if I was caught between a rock and a hard place and I constantly looked for answers to financial and professional improvement locally, to no avail. Finally, one day in the midst of the peak of social unrest we decided that migration could be an option.

I had returned home because I wanted to live at home and settle, start a family and nurse my fellow citizens who had the greatest need. It was hard to get to that point but I truly felt that I was a part of a team that provided a service that gave our patients the opportunity to live longer and enjoy a better quality of life. Unfortunately, I gave almost everything. I felt morally good to be a part of that health team, but socially and economically, things were changing. There were also plans to narrow the high school exams to uniquely fit the Caribbean population. Now this sounded good to the politicians. However, I saw it as limiting the job market for my children. If, and when they graduated from high school here (in Jamaica) and wanted to live elsewhere in the world, they would have to take more qualifying exams to prove their ability to function in that new work environment. Remembering my own experience, I did not think that would be fair to them. To my husband and me, our daily living expenses were exceeding our salaries, and there was no vision of improvement, and so migration was seen as a possible solution to our strife.

I felt that our children deserved better. They would have attended good schools, but, who knows? We probably would not have been able to afford college and that would have been devastating to us as parents. Hopefully, at least we would be able to adequately feed and clothe our children. As one can imagine, none of these decisions were made spontaneously. We were dedicated, patriotic adults who had to face reality and decide to live as patriots and definitely not survive, or migrate and try to start again in a foreign environment, attempting to make it better for our children by exposing them to more opportunities and hopefully a better chance at social mobility.

My marriage was far from perfect. We continued with our strife. However, we both decided to move as a family. I never gave separation a thought. My husband's moods continued and together we continued with plans to move. We transferred these issues to another continent, with me not even able to admit that I could have made it on my own as a single mother. We continued to pretend to people that we were a happy family.

GRANDMOTHER'S STAMINA

On April 16th 2010 my son called me. 'Mom, what anniversary are we celebrating today?' he asked cheerily. I did not want to appear demented. Quietly I thought…what are we celebrating today? My parents would have been married 68 years ago, but my father died over a year ago…and so I did not think that was the answer…anyway I was sure that their date was April 14th. My patience was stretching and spontaneously my brain stopped trying to remember, to get to the point I asked him to tell me what we were celebrating.

'Today marks 26 years since we left Jamaica to come to the United States. How could you forget that day?'

'*How could I indeed*', I thought. I have not forgotten the year, but I have to think to remember the date.

'So much has happened since that date eh Mom?' he stated fondly.

"Yes son…so much…do you remember when we….'

Then I drifted off to relate some experience either with the travel preparations or with the actual trip.

'We have come a long way Mom…but it was for the good of all of us'… personally I have never doubted that it was the right decision for the family. I am not a fortune teller, but I am sure that if we remained on our beautiful tropical island, we would have continued to struggle. Many people have since asked us how we could possibly have left all the white sand beaches, cool tropical breezes and lovely tropical fruit, to start life over in a new culture and almost foreign environment. I say 'almost foreign environment', because we were raised under a British colonial system that was different to the American way of life. Anyway, I always respond with a smile and say honestly…

'You cannot eat the beauty…you need other things to survive'.

The time it took us to prepare to move and until we actually moved was about two and a half to three years. There was a job vacancy in a small town in Arkansas and I was offered the job. I knew enough to be aware of the fact that it must be 'small town' with many added hidden variables if they were recruiting me and not a local candidate. We chose to move to Arkansas instead of New York or Baltimore. Those were large cities, and we thought that it would be wiser to get our children transitioned and integrated into a small community than a large city. We were informed enough to be aware of the history of this Southern state however, we had already enlightened our children to the existence of racial hatred and discrimination in the world. We also told our children that legally there was now a law in place to combat the incidents of preventing unequal opportunity for all citizens. We tried not to create fear in them, but instead to remind them repeatedly why, despite all this, we had to leave our home and live in this new community.

When the time to pack our belongings arrived, it was difficult to select what we needed to take in addition to our clothes and travel documents. I packed card and board games, school reports, schoolbooks with written work that our children had done for the most recent semester, some textbooks (like math and English texts). Of course these were British and slightly different in style to the American equivalent, and so we discarded these on arrival, to allow the children to get accustomed to and utilize the new methods. We thought that continued access to their former textbooks would have them comparing both and that would create more confusion for them.

The Jamaican government was experiencing a 'brain drain'. The economy was bad, jobs were scarce and people were seeking employment overseas. In order to make travel unattractive, a limit was placed on how much foreign exchange travelers could leave the island with…it was a grand total of $50 per adult. That did not impede us because we already had a plan, and it worked well for us. However, we were far from rich and we had to travel with more belongings than usual in order to reduce our initial spending on arrival to this country. We knew that I would be working a week after arrival, but my husband would be unemployed and we did not know for how long…so we had to be frugal.

My parents and maternal grandmother understood why we had to leave our home. My parents were now age 67 and 69 and they we fully independent. My grandmother, who lived with us, was 89 and independent, but she was frail with congestive heart failure. Initially, it was the most difficult thing to tell her that we were planning to leave. She could live with my mother and this would not have been a problem, but I felt that I was deserting her at a time when she needed me. I was pleasantly surprised when I told her of our plans to migrate, she said…

'Ms. Kathleen, it is time you were rewarded for all the hard work that you have been doing…you have had to work too hard here and the children will definitely get better opportunities where you are going. I love your mother like the daughter I never had…so do not worry about us, we will be OK. I will not live to see you return, but you all deserve better. God go with you my dear child.'

Her eyes were dry, her words were again correct and I wept silently as I hugged her and confirmed that it was again time to move on.

HERE WE ARE

We packed our belongings into four large suitcases. This was all that we would have access to for the next month to six weeks until I got paid, so we had to be frugal. My parents drove us to the airport and saying goodbye to them was extremely sad. My emotions were mixed. We were leaving home because remaining was not an option. Here we were with these two small children in our care, our son had just turned twelve the month before and my daughter was six years old. Failure was not an option either. So, looking back, I can say now that although I was sad, I was cautiously looking forward to starting over. I saw this as an opportunity for all of us to fulfill our dreams.

I prayed that our children would be able to cope with the transition. They were both doing well academically. Our son had successfully completed almost two semesters at his new high school. He had successfully passed the dreaded Common Entrance exam the previous summer and was accepted by the high school that was his first choice. In Jamaica, in order to qualify for free tuition in the high school system, one had to sit a qualifying exam and one had approximately two chances at this, beginning at age eleven. The disadvantage however was that there were thousands of children sitting this exam for few available vacant slots in the schools. This created fierce competition with parents seeking the best means to coach their children and the schools narrowing their acceptance criteria, in order to accept children into the few available spaces. It was what I refer to as another Third World dilemma. We were told afterwards that 35,000 children took that exam and only approximately 7,000 school vacancies existed. What was grossly unfair was that children, who were well prepared academically, still were excluded from getting a good education, because there were not enough vacancies in the choice schools. We were also informed that our son missed a Government scholarship by less than 10 points. This would have meant free education plus free books and uniforms. We were all very happy to hear that and we cautiously hoped that he would be able to cope with the transition to a new culture.

Our daughter, on the other hand, was growing into a very outspoken, no nonsense child. She grasped ideas quickly, she read well, she spoke her mind easily…sometimes to our embarrassment. She had completed a year and almost two semesters at a private Preparatory School. She could read, write cursively, do simple arithmetic, her vocabulary was developing well. She was doing well academically, for her age. We both saw our children as being very loving, and well balanced. My son was shyer emotionally and my daughter was the opposite. Emotional stability was also infused, I thought, from regular interaction with their grandparents. Again I cautiously prayed that they, our children, would be able to cope with this move and that they would continue to accept our rules in a new culture. I cannot describe my husband's emotions in detail, except that he seemed to be coping well and he too expressed hope that we would all be able to cope. He never shared his fears, but this was not new, as he was never vocally emotional.

Personally, my emotions could be described as being apprehensive but hopeful. I was apprehensive because I was moving to a culture that was new, foreign and maybe hostile. I was going to be working in and taking qualifying exams in this world. I would have to think, relate, interact, and rationalize in this new society. The future and success of this move for the family seemed to be dependent on how I coped with the transition.

I would continue to share at home, my experiences and how I coped, especially during some anxious moments. We had to be cautious with what we said, we had to remember the history of the town, we had to be street smart, but polite. We had to remember that we were foreign and black, and place that in perspective, sometimes as to how different social groups viewed us. I held firm to my faith in God and the vivid knowledge of conditions that we had left behind. Failing was not an option and returning home was not a part of our plan.

We landed at Little Rock airport in April 1984, and we were met by a friendly young driver who explained that he worked at the hospital and that he was sent to collect us and transport us to our new home. The arrangements included staying at a motel for a week until we found accommodation near to work.

All that I remember from our drive to our new small town home was that there were several broken pine trees. We were told that the last winter was severe and that the weight of the snow had broken the tree branches and done extensive damage. I made a mental note as I smiled politely.

'Winter is severe, winter clothes will have to be substantial'.

We were taken to the small twenty-six bed hospital where I was to work. Here we were introduced to the Director of Nursing. The Hospital Administrator, who had hired me, was an inpatient; he unfortunately, had a recent heart attack. I made another quick mental note…

'Hold the gift box of Jamaican cigars'.

Also within this building was a small six or ten bed Nursing Home that was staffed separately. People appeared to be friendly, and greeted us warmly. We were invited to have lunch at the hospital cafeteria and then we were transported to our motel, on the edge of town.

The motel was located at a truck stop. We went there to eat our first breakfast the next morning. In order to call home to assure my parents that we had arrived safely, we all walked to the truck stop to use the payphone to make a 'collect call'. Collectively, we all knew that this would not have been our choice of accommodation, but we accepted that it was free and temporary.

Our first priority was signing the necessary employment contracts, finding somewhere to live and registering the children in school. I agreed to be paid $9.00 an hour, and I would work any shift. We had previously estimated that we could survive at that pay scale. I assumed that everyone was paid at that rate.

Accommodation was not available. The block of apartments across the street from work, was now unavailable. Our search now extended further from the hospital, but we had no transportation. Our stay at the motel was extended for another week and so was my starting date to work. On one occasion a realtor/car dealership owner contacted us personally and told us that he heard that we needed somewhere to live and that he had just the 'home' that we would like. We thanked him, made an appointment to meet with him, and thought that finally, we were moving forward. Looking back, this was small town rural USA, everyone knew that we were in town, everyone knew our movements and employment plans.

The 'home' turned out to be a trailer behind a nearby supermarket. I was polite but furious. We declined his generous offer, sought a lift back to the hospital and told the people responsible for relocating us that I had never lived in a trailer and that I did not plan doing so now. I also told them that I could see a vacant apartment in the building across the street, and if they were having problems with relocating us then probably, the entire employment contract could be reconsidered. I chose my words very carefully, I did not want us to be sent back home, but I was not prepared to live in the side of town across the railway tract where obviously society had designated for 'my kind'.

CULTURE SHOCK

In a remarkable short time, an empty furnished apartment a block from the hospital was identified, and we moved in. The Director of Nursing remarked to me that she finally realized that 'it was not who you were, that was important, but whom you knew'. I could have told her that also. This was the start of our new life in this small town. We registered the children in schools that were within a mile from our new home and they started school in the middle of the term.

Our son started in the 7th grade, and because of his height, the football coach soon suggested that he should be on the team, and was obviously surprised when he declined. He was a year younger than his classmates, and we had to constantly reassure him and boost his morale each day as he learned how to interact with his new school mates. It must have been hell for him, because they wasted no time informing him that he was too young to be in their groups. Being academically sound did not help either. As parents we struggled and prayed that he would not forget that there was nothing wrong with doing well in school. God answered our prayers because he took his work seriously and he worked well. He had to cope with puberty, hormones, being a new teenager, as well as making new friends.

Our daughter, who was six going on seven, was placed with a group of children who were just starting school. This was done although I had traveled with her current school work, and shared this with the principal. He just said, in an unbelieving tone…

'So this is your daughter's work eh? Kids her age are just starting school'… he told me. I did not argue as he took her to the group of new children having their first school experience. She did not remain here as she demonstrated that she could indeed read and write. She was taken to two other grades and settled I think, in the second grade. She too was ignored by her class mates who called her a baby. So, although she sat with them for classes, she was not included in their games. This was a situation that we had to work very hard at, in order to maintain her vibrant, cheerful spirit. We constantly had to reassure our children that we had to do this in order to move on and create a better life for us all. It was a very difficult time. We were counselors, prayer partners, home tutors and just plain supporting parents to these bewildered children.

Soon after we moved into our apartment, news that we were Presbyterian spread, and someone from that denomination visited us and invited us to church. We found a new church family and people were very friendly. The children were shown love and they, in return, began to play and interact well, displaying their true characters and we looked forward to sessions at church and with this new group of friends. I must admit that I was very cautious, and prayed unceasingly for their safe return if ever they went on outings.

There were times when I had to braid my daughter's hair and, at her request, pin the braids up on her head. She told me afterwards, that a bully would pull her hair and that she did not want to get into a fight with him. My husband and I had to meet with one of our son's teachers because she labeled him as being very conceited, because he could do his class work, she actually told him so in class. This was her misconception, and so after meeting with her and really talking through what she expected and what our son was actually doing, she began to see that it was more of a cultural difference that we easily explained.

We were advised that the children could travel on the school bus and that they would have school lunch. We found out afterwards that they qualified for the free lunch, according to the family's income. I was resentful at first, because I did not want us to be labeled as receiving aid as soon as we arrived, and I was actually working. However, we agreed as we felt that refusing could have been misinterpreted as our not wanting our children to interact with others.

We arrived in the USA during an election year and we were bewildered as people knocked on our door, shook our hand and said,

'We appreciate you'. I had no idea what they meant.

Our social and cultural transition seemed to be going well. However, we realized that we were resented by one group because we socialized with another. We were familiar with the Presbyterian Church's worship format, making us traitors and downright strange in the eyes of the black community. We were not familiar with anything in Hollywood, we did not understand American football, and we had a strange accent.

'Y'all talk funny', people said, through clenched teeth, their natural method of communicating. Sometimes they called us 'Yankees'. When we were alone as a family, we would have a hearty laugh, but we realized that we had to tread on thin ice, because interaction was going to take longer than we expected.

My children, Ann (age 7) and Maurice (age 12); their first school photographs in Arkansas in 1984

SMALL TOWN

Well here we were in the United States of America. The children were in school and were gradually coping with the transition. My husband had difficulty finding employment, and later (through the grapevine) we learned that they said that he was too qualified. The children were transported to school on the school bus…and after about a month they were told that they were on the 'wrong' bus, and that they needed to wait for another to pick them up. We agreed and as usual, we waited for the bus to arrive. It was late. That afternoon they told us that they were both late for school. They also said that the bus went through extremely depressed areas of the small town, and that all the children on this bus were African American. The children were upset that they were late for school and that there were clearly two routes and two distinct groups of passengers classified according to race. Although our apartment was not located in the slum, sadly, the community had already aligned us to where its members felt that we belonged. My son chose to walk to school and when we bought a car, my husband would transport them to and from school. A church member also offered to take them to school when we were unable to do so.

Soon we were advised of towns that we should avoid driving through after dark. We also saw some men who wore KKK inscribed on their belt buckles. At work, I was referred to as 'that nigger' by a few patients. Let me hasten to add that there were people who were very kind to us and who never hesitated to reassure us that we could depend on them for any necessary assistance. I knew that we could not remain in this community. I knew that soon we would be caught deep in the mire of segregation and I also silently feared the outcome of any confrontation. The summary of my status is as follows:-

I was employed to work as an RN with a temporary license that expired after a year. Future employment meant that I had to sit and pass the Nursing State Board Exam before the end of the year.

The hospital was sold and was under new management. The Director of Nursing with whom I worked had resigned. Staff was reassigned.

I was one of the two black RNs employed; we were both from Jamaica, and both with British qualifications.

I had tried unsuccessfully to work elsewhere.

I had a professional disagreement with the person in charge of the lab. I was told that I did not know my job, as I successfully argued before a group of hospital managers, that blood was not satisfactorily stored and therefore a specific unit was unsuitable for transfusion.

I had thirteen years of nursing experience under my belt; I had certification in Midwifery, Dialysis and Renal Transplant and Nursing Administration. I knew that I had to move on and seek employment elsewhere, but first I had to take that qualifying exam for a permanent license.

Reviewing material for the State Exam must have been one of the hardest tasks that I tackled up to that period of my life. Mentally I had to reason/ rationalize like an American. I had to fast forward my brain to think and reason from a developed world, privatized Health Care perspective, one in which patients had the right to do what they wanted, to expect what they asked for and if it was not provided, then there was a legal system that could demand it. I am racking my brain at this point to find a suitable example to illustrate the subtle difference, but I cannot.

I sat with review material for hours at a time. I was frustrated and angry...

'What if I failed?' I would wail...

'I cannot do this!' After every such moment, I would stop, and remember that others had done it before and that alone was proof that it was not an impossible task. Well, I took the exam in Texas, because if I passed I could also work there, if I failed, I would still be able to work in Arkansas until my temporary license expired. No one at the hospital knew that I was taking this exam, and so when I passed, I told no one.

As a family, we were elated! It meant that now I could apply to other states for work and that many would give me a license based on the results from the Texas State Board exam. I was offered a job at the Tulane Medical Center in New Orleans, Louisiana. I would be paid more than twice my current salary, my years of experience were recognized, and my job would be in the dialysis and kidney transplant unit.

I was happy, and the children were ecstatic, my husband was thrilled. It was a big city, there would be more opportunities and it really was time to leave Arkansas. I tendered my resignation, expressing my gratitude for all that they had done for us, we also told our church family that we were leaving. We made plans to attach a small trailer with all of our earthly belongings to our small Chevette and to those who did not need to know, and who insisted on asking…

‘Where y'all heading?’ I smiled and replied…

‘Further south’.

ON THE ROAD AGAIN

The title of this Country and Western song is appropriate for our family at this stage of our adventure. It was May 1985, and we were on the road to New Orleans, Louisiana. When I think about it, we had left Jamaica with four suitcases...now we had upgraded our status to a small U-Haul trailer attached to our small car. All of our belongings, including a few house plants were on board. I have no sense of direction, worse if I am given Cardinal signs. So I was comfortable with knowing that we were headed for Louisiana, without getting the details of the trip. My husband loves to drive, and this was easy for him. The one small annoying detail is...he never takes a direct route...so we went from Arkansas through Mississippi into Louisiana. The children were comfortable in the back of the car with blankets, pillows and a large comforter. They dozed on and off as we traveled into the night. I stayed awake, for moral support and as an extra pair of eyes, just in case the driver's eyes were strained. With no drivers license however, I could not help to drive if it became necessary.

During the first part of the road trip, a fearful thought crossed my mind. My God, here we were in transit! If we had an accident no one would know who we were, or who our next- of- kin was, we could have been removed form the face of the earth with no one missing us. The family in Jamaica knew that we were moving, but I did not share with them the exact travel date, I felt then, that they would only worry unnecessarily. I did not share my fear with anyone however, as my husband would probably have taken it personally, that I was referring to his driving, and it was too dreadful a thought to share with the children. So I did what I had become very good at, I prayed earnestly to God for our safety.

We left the state of Arkansas with a sigh relief. As we crossed into Mississippi, there was a loud repetitive banging sound that seemed to be coming from the trailer. In the dead of night we pulled into a gas station in

Tallulah, Mississippi, to get some help. Speech impediment again created communication problems, but we clearly understood the final diagnosis...

'Y'all wheel is broke', the sleepy, attendant said through a full lip of chewing tobacco.

'Y'all need to ask Bubba at the truck stop for help', was his kind response to our desperate...

'Can you fix it?'

So once again we were destined to go to another truck stop, to wait until morning, find Bubba, (whose real name now escapes my memory) and ask him to repair the wheel on this ill fated trailer with all our belongings. Things worked well...once again I felt that I made contact with God and that He was indeed following us. I know that He was aware of the importance of this trip, and that we honestly needed help, His help. We were delayed for a while as the part for the wheel was replaced and our load appeared secure and safe for us to complete our trip.

The children were awake for the final daylight miles of the trip and they were enamored with the lush green farms, the livestock grazing and the change in scenery as we obviously moved through different socio-economic communities. It was a good lesson in Social Studies for them. By now you can guess that we are not traveling on the Interstate, but gladly rolling along on the scenic routes.

We finally enter the state of Louisiana and the difference in the road surface is the first thing that we noticed. It is not a smooth ride at all. Someone said that it reminded them of our roads in Jamaica. That is not complimentary. We drove over the Causeway and gasped at the size of Lake Pontchartrain. We gazed at the vast expanse of swamp land, famously called 'Bayous' in that part of the world. It was a new sight, a new town. We drove to the West Bank, where we would meet a friend to find an apartment. The West Bank was called the West Bank, but it was actually, east of the Mississippi River. That certainly did not help my confusion with directions.

We settled into a three bedroom Town House. The children said that it felt more like home to have a garden and their own room. We were all tired but thrilled that we had tackled the road trip. I renamed the U-Haul trailer, You-Haul. We had left Arkansas and we were about to start the second part of our relocation. No one at this time could have imagined that we would settle in the Bayou country for the next twenty years.

NEW ORLEANS

While we were in Arkansas, my sister wanted to visit. I reluctantly mentioned that the apartment only had two bedrooms, and she casually said…

'I could always stay at a hotel.'

'Yes' I thought…'at the truck stop'.

Eventually, we agreed that she would visit us in New Orleans soon after we got there. We had not seen each other for about 3 years and it was wonderful! I think that I had a week off prior to starting my new job and the children were on summer holidays. When she arrived, it was just in time to explore the city, with her niece and nephew; they were all craving to go somewhere and as a trio they bonded well. The children were old enough to enjoy and appreciate new things, and discover new places. They went to the Audubon zoo, they toured the city, sailed on a River boat, got sick together with new food, enjoyed the French Quarter, they listened to jazz, to name a few activities. They had a wonderful time. The children were happy to be in a new, large, developed city, and my sister simply fell in love with New Orleans. People were friendly and the pace was slower than other American cities, but brisker than our previous stop. Friends advised us…

'Do not drink the tap water, it will turn your teeth brown'.

So, we did not drink the tap water. At work I met a few more Jamaican nurses, some of whom were previously in Arkansas. Our stories were almost similar, and always with conviction, each would conclude…

'I had to move away from there, as soon as it became possible'.

Work was wonderful. I was working for a progressive organization. I was back in my former specialty, kidney dialysis and transplant. The patients, the world over, had similar personalities. They were well informed about their illness and they understood the important role that dialysis played in their survival. It was good to be able to work and not have to worry about the availability of supplies, or patients not coming for their treatment because they had no transportation. Family members were supportive and if they were not, then the social services provided assistance. These were some of the differences between the delivery of care to patients in a developed country and in a Third World country. Poorer countries did not have money to pay for support services. I enjoyed working at this facility. I felt that there was room for professional growth. I also fantasized that if I remained here long enough, my son, who was five years older than his sister, could go to this college and probably qualify for tuition assistance, because of the fact that I worked for the organization.

We settled into life in New Orleans. We became members of a Presbyterian Church very near to our home. The members were not very friendly. We kept going however, determined that we needed to attend church for our mental survival. Sometimes I would leave the services angry as everyone greeted their peers like old 'buddies', but we never really felt as if we were a part of the true church family. Even after attending for several years sometimes that feeling never changed. I continued attending that church, because I was Presbyterian, and because I truly felt that the church represented the community and it would be no different anywhere else. Then I thought that I needed to go to worship with a group, and to be replenished for the week by singing hymns and interacting with a group of people with one common belief. Interestingly enough, as I get older, and continue to learn life through my experiences, I have become very contented with discovering God's presence all around me. I have felt very uncomfortable with some of the strong traditional judgments that some preachers teach from the pulpit.

Well all the other aspects of life seemed to be going well for us. The children were in school and doing well. My husband decided that he wanted to further his education and it seemed to be a good plan. I co-signed on his first student loan, as I was the only one working. He started at a junior college and then transferred to a four -year program. There were some things for me that I felt needed changing. I had to get my drivers license, and take charge of my car. I also longed to own a home and I had no idea how to even start the process. I worried that as the sole bread-winner, if anything happened to me, there was no life insurance and no money would be available to continue a stable life and to educate our children.

We were a few steps ahead socially, but we had no security, and I was uncomfortable with being in that position. Then, we talked through potential problems as a couple. Subconsciously, however, I decided to resolve them. It was clear to me that my husband's focus was on his education and our other family problems were not considered a priority.

NEW ORLEANS (CONTD.)

Today I remember the last eight weeks and the wonderful visit that I experienced with my sister. The older I get the more I am aware of how important our friendship is. It took us many years to get to this point. We fought like demons as children and there certainly was sibling rivalry…but we have matured and with time, we now love and respect each other. We talked about our feelings as children and who in the family we thought understood us, and whom we did not like and why. It was interesting to hear my sister say…

'You say that you felt as if you were always in my shadow.' (I had asked her to read the work on my memoirs to this point).

'But I was jealous of you because I thought that Daddy preferred you and that was one reason why I always got angry and delivered swift justice in a quick slap'.

I always felt dumb following my sister…well we cleared that delusion up once and for all, during this recent visit. As a mother, I wish that my two children will realize how important it is to be close to each other, regardless of their different opinions.

Let me refocus on my life in New Orleans. From 1985 until 1998 my life focused primarily around my children and their education. I also continued to be very defensive of my husband who worked briefly, and who went to school for educational and career development. I also had the opportunity to improve professionally. As a family, we felt that we were constantly receiving Divine guidance and protection.

Our son went onto a Junior High School, in Eighth grade, for the first year in New Orleans, he did very well, and he graduated as Valedictorian in 1986. We went to that graduation ceremony unaware of his accomplishment. His Home Room teacher's face beamed as she said,

'Y'all must be very proud of your son'.

'Yes' I replied. 'We are'.

I said this quickly and moved on, I did not want my husband to enter into a long conversation with her at this time, as seating was scarce. We were surprised when the awards were announced and his name was called. I felt that we were continuing on a good path with our children, and I thanked God that our son had adjusted to the educational system despite all the interruptions in his young life. He went to one of the best High Schools in New Orleans and was well prepared for college. We heard of this school purely by accident, as someone bragged about the school's success and we soon found out later that many of the City's leaders and top college graduates were former students.

Our daughter went into third grade at a nearby elementary school. For fourth grade she moved to the middle school and when the area in which we lived was rezoned she moved back to the elementary school which was now changed to accept students through to grade six. She went to the same junior high school as her brother. Area rezoning seemed to dictate that she should continue at this same junior high school, which was now changed to accept students through to grade twelve, then she successfully passed the entrance exam to our choice high school and, like her brother, was well prepared for college. There was a lot of rezoning of districts that occurred and it could have negatively affected our children, but somehow it always worked to their advantage.

In 1987, we purchased our first home. My sister kindly lent us the money for our five percent deposit, and we qualified for the loan. Although no financial contribution came from my husband, it was our first home and both of our names were on the deed for this piece of real estate below sea level.

New Orleans was noted as the 'City that care forgot', it was also a fun loving, party city and was famous for parades, festivals and endless celebrations, the most famous being, Mardi Gras. I had the pleasure of experiencing Mardi Gras in 'the Hood', in 2005, not knowing at the time that it would be my last. My friend, who lived in New Orleans for many years, was amazed that I had not seen this side of Mardi Gras, and so with four others we went off early to the site where the Zulu Parade floats started. Everyone greeted each other as long time friends, stories were shared easily, food was exchanged with delight, the potency of drinks was respected, costumes were admired, and new friends were made. The floats were elaborately decorated with the tons of colorful beads, brightly painted coconuts, and the largest and wildest collection of toys and stuffed animals. The toys were tossed to the children who lived in the 'Government housing projects,' and they were gleefully received by children and adults. As the parade drove through the less depressed areas of the city, the 'throws' consisted mainly of beads…again to the cheering crowd's delight.

On any day, jazz music was played on the radio stations, from speakers in some of the parks, from the street corners in the French Quarter. The city literally 'grew on you'. Many people who lived there would say,

'I came here for one visit and I never left.'

We would visit the French Quarter and enjoy listening to music, watch people of all ages, dance tirelessly to the constant melodious sounds, and we would dine at the endless restaurants enjoying the cuisine. Needless to say, most of the food was fried but it was delightfully seasoned. The music had an influence on me…where ever I was the urge to dance was almost spontaneous. In this city I grew to appreciate jazz and to keenly listen to the blend of drums, saxophones, clarinets to name a few of the instruments. I love the sound of plain old Honky-Tonk music on the piano, and I had illusions of playing like that when I retired. Needless to say I would first have to learn how to play the piano. It required strict discipline, and with my moods and duo personalities (Gemini) I have the books to teach myself, but carving out time everyday, has proven to be downright impossible.

We spent many weekend afternoons sitting on the balcony of the Riverwalk restaurants, gazing at the illuminated Mississippi River Bridge and watching the river traffic silently glide up and down this river. Each tugboat pilot had his own mission, pushing barges filled with grain or fuel to destinations that were unknown to the fascinated spectators. After many stressful days of demanding work, I would drive onto the ferry at the end of Canal Street. I would pray for a safe journey and I would try not to acknowledge that this matchbox on water (the ferry), could indeed collide with a large tanker and sink, or could sink even without colliding with anything. My fears would always subside as I watched the city's skyline disappear and we docked on the river's west bank where our home was located. Near to the dock was a quiet pub that served delicious sweet potato chips that I enjoyed many an evening with a glass of Gin and Ginger Ale, or Cabernet, and absorbed the soft sounds of blues or brass band or jazz.

This was one aspect of life and it was lovely. At home, the reality was that I had to deal with supporting the family, coping with a husband who sometimes appeared to be exerting control over my income. I also had to appear to be competent and sane at work and try to remain current with my clinical skills, and to function competently. I had to reassure the children that we would meet our goals as a family. Together we talked about college for our children, but there were no funds and it seemed to be almost impossible. Once again, we discovered that it was possible and slowly the pieces of our lives' great 'jig saw puzzle' fitted together beautifully, and with faith, higher education became a reality.

My parents, Fitzgerald and Enid Wilson on one of their visits to Algiers, Louisiana.

Me, in 1997, at the lakeside, in New Orleans.

OUR NEW HOME (contd.)

We liked New Orleans. The way of life was 'laid back", the people were friendly and in a way it could be compared to life in Jamaica. I was surprised when I went to the Water Office and was directed to 'take a number'. That was a method of crowd control that was frequently used in Kingston…and it rarely worked. Here however, with more staff and a less frustrated crowd, it seemed to work well. It was always said that New Orleanians needed no excuse to party or to have a parade. That was true. It was good if you were with the partying crowd, but again frustrating if you were not.

I worked at the Tulane Medical Center and did well. I liked what I was doing. It was a privately owned facility and emphasis on cost and profit was always important for survival of the organization. I remained at this facility for three and a half years and I decided to leave because I yearned for professional development. I received verbal recognition, but training opportunities were few…for me. I watched as some of my colleagues moved forward…but I could not get my 'foot on the rung of that ladder' for educational growth. I wanted to learn more, to move away from Dialysis Nursing, to work with more acutely ill patients.

Looking back at my life at this point, my son was now almost a senior in high school, we had bought our first home, my husband was still in school, not employed, and my daughter was doing well in junior high school. I owned the family car, but did not have a license. I was timid to drive. I was repaying the loan to my sister, (the loan for the deposit on our home). I also had the 'dutiful wife' mentality…every payday I would cash my check and give the money to my husband to take home. My Third World mentality instructed me to send it home to safety. I took on a second job in order to save for an emergency fund for the family. As a couple, discussion and planning issues were never easy, and so I would go ahead and do what I thought was necessary for the family.

My husband, I thought, did have mental control over the family and there was always a conflict. I bought life insurance and contributed to a private annuity fund. I felt that if either of us died, the house could be paid for, and whoever survived would not have to worry about paying a mortgage. I also felt that with us getting older, we needed to think about saving for retirement... hence the annuity fund seemed to be a practical solution. My husband began to express doubt of my loyalty, and he said that I was planning to have him killed, by insuring both of us. He wanted none of it. At first I ignored him... it was too bizarre, but he insisted that the insurance be cancelled and so I did just that. We would go out as a family, but somehow we would always end up fussing about something and gradually, I did not socialize. I could not cope with the discontent and quarrels that erupted, sometimes for simple reasons. My parents visited us every year, for the first few years they visited separately and they provided a good opportunity for the children to reconnect with them. It was a relief for me because at first, we acted like a united family and enjoyed each others company. Later on, this would also change.

Well...one day I was getting 'driving lessons' on parallel parking from my husband. This was a necessary part of learning to drive. It was frustrating. I could not get the distance between the curb and the wheels correct and, needless to say, the lessons were prematurely discontinued. At work, I asked a former marine who was telling us that his son had recently received his driver's license,

'Did he have to parallel park?'...

'No, they do not seem to do that anymore'.

Well I started to see the light! The following week, I went for and passed my driving test and got my license. The smile on that license was huge, one of the few licenses with a good photograph.

Now I needed access to my car, and the conflict got worse. Quietly I insisted that instead of being driven to work, I could drop off my husband on campus sometimes and have the car to take the children out. I felt that this would give them a new freedom. We could now spend some quiet time at the malls or at picnics on the levees. We went to the movies as a threesome and spoke freely about plans, hopes, likes and dislikes. My children did complain about their father's behavior, and they were not happy. Sometimes they even suggested how he could find employment while on campus, but he responded that would be a distraction from his goal, and so he disagreed with these suggestions.

There was a lot of turmoil and discontent and still, we remained together, as a family. Looking back, we were a dysfunctional family for years. Divorce, however, never seemed to be an option. I changed jobs and went to work for the Veterans Administration Medical Center. Having worked at the Government hospitals in Jamaica, the beauracracy that many people complained about, within this organization, was not new to me, and coping with it was easy. I started in the Surgical Intensive Care Unit. There was an official orientation period, and I would have a mentor with me for a given period, or until we were both assured that I was clinically competent to function independently. There were educators and a library on site. Within the organization, this provided immense study opportunity and reference material to anyone who needed it. I was elated. It was immensely stressful, but I was willing to face the challenge. It meant that after working twelve hour shifts, I would go home with reference material to read and study. I felt that I was now able to be a part of a new aspect of nursing with a very progressive group of colleagues and I was thrilled.

Our son graduated from high school in 1989. Prior to his final year I encouraged him to find out everything about scholarships and financing for his education. He applied to numerous colleges and finally decided that it would be cheaper to remain in the state, but he confided that if he remained in state, he wanted to attend the best college. That became a reality. We spent many late hours looking at the total cost of his education and planning how to pay for it. Finally it became a reality, he received a few small scholarships, he got student loans and we calculated his other expenses to the last dollar. To make this payment possible, that total was divided by twelve, the twelve months of the year ...that gave me the total that I need to save to meet this new expense. At this point our son was the pioneer. We had come a long way in a new world. We had constantly preached to our children the importance of a good education for social mobility, and now he was on the threshold of a new chapter of his life. So again, with faith, a steady job and health, we moved forward.

FALL 1989

I firmly believe in the bible verses of Proverbs chapter 3, verses 5 and 6, The King James' version *(Trust in the Lord with all thine heart; and lean not unto thine own understanding. In all thy ways acknowledge Him, and He shall direct thy paths.)* My elderly neighbor in Jamaica gave me those words before I migrated and I continually thank his memory for that gift. It was one of the best gifts that I have ever received. I have had to believe in those verses daily and now I use them for reassurance. There are times when I forget that I am not able to resolve all my problems and, during those times, I remember the verses and literally submit to God.

When our son started college, I feared that maybe I would be unable to find enough money to meet the predicted balances. There were many rough times, but each time the bills were paid. New textbooks, unexpected expenses, and the regular annual 10% tuition fees increase were all taken care of, only by the grace of God.

My daughter successfully passed the high school entrance exam and she started high school in 1990. That worked well for both of them, because they repeatedly told each other that seniors did not 'speak' to freshmen. She coped well at high school and appeared to make many friends. Many of her friends from elementary school continued through to high school and there seemed to be more continuity for her psychological transition to college. She also seemed to be coping very well with school and I felt that she was at an advantage, because once the problems were met and resolved from her brother's experiences, the path was paved for her to follow.

Looking back there were many unpredictable problems during 1989 and 1993. I started my new job at the VAMC (Veterans Affairs Medical Center) and passed my physical. Late 1989 an annual routine physical exam was due. I went to have my EKG exam, and the technician was trying her best to make conversation, and she asked if I had family here in the US with me. I thought at first that she was being nosey and I said

'No'.

When I saw a copy of my test, I realized why she asked me that question. Here I was saving lives in SICU and I am holding an abnormal EKG result, my own. Suddenly my knowledge freezes and I am unable to concentrate on what I am seeing. There are definitely abnormal changes and the narrative confirms 'Ischemic changes…M.I.…age unknown.'(Or other words with the same meaning). I had no chest pain, none that I could remember, it must have been a 'silent M.I.' There is such a diagnosis. I worked well with the Cardiologists and cardio-vascular surgeons, and so I showed one of them my results and he said casually…

'I would not worry Kathleen, they probably did not place the leads correctly, and that would alter the results'.

Now I worked with this stuff, and I doubt that I would have overlooked misplaced leads on my chest…but I had it repeated and the results were the same. I was very afraid. I had an Echocardiogram that showed minimal abnormalities. I had no symptoms. I needed to have a Stress Test and I hesitated. I was too afraid to have it done. I was too afraid to face the results, I fretted for my family, who all depended on my good health for their survival. My daughter looked at me one day and said, plainly…

'How can you hesitate to take the test? How will you know the extent of any abnormality if you do not have it done?'

Like a true 'parent', I said…

'I am very scared of what I will hear.'

'Mom we are here for you, but first, promise me that you will get this done as soon as possible'.

So, I did. I had the Stress Test and fortunately, no intervention was required.

As a pledge to myself, I stopped taking the elevator to the sixth floor to work and I used the stairs always…every work day that meant going up and down six flights of stairs at least four times. I thought…well if I was going to get another heart attack…it might as well happen at work. If not, I would strengthen my cardiovascular function and use the time on the stairs as quiet time, to clear my mind also. I knew that I was doing a lot and working very hard, but I had no choice, so I kept going.

My husband transferred to a four-year college to an Accounting program. He joined a work study program and got a job. We continued to bicker over the car and its use, and in 1993, he bought a new car…he resolved that problem.

Our son graduated from Tulane in May 1993. He did very well. He had decided that he was ready to live out of the state, and that he wanted to go to medical school. He successfully sat his MCAT exam. Four programs including Dartmouth College, which was his first choice, accepted him. As a family we all truly believed, that the student loans would be large, but graduating from Dartmouth Medical School would surely enable him to commence a career that could provide a steady income to repay the loans.

So once again the expenses were calculated to the last dollar and temporary accommodation was promised from a friend of a faculty member. In September our son and a fellow Tulane graduate set off for New Hampshire in the friend's Volkswagen Jetta. They had a hearty breakfast, food for the trip, money for emergencies, unlimited prayers and safety advice and I shed enough tears for both mothers.

LOOKING BACK AT A DYSFUNCTIONAL PERIOD

Last Thursday after the landscaper had cut the grass, I decided that the shrubs needed pruning. I pruned with zeal, I raked the surrounding areas to my satisfaction in the boiling sun, and I watered the garden and myself. It felt great, I was exhausted and my mind was at peace. I had to comment...

'My God Kathleen, ten years ago, this peace would have been inconceivable.'

Mentally I concluded that all wounds do heal with time. As you have guessed, here, I digress. Looking back, over the years, so much has happened, so many things have changed and so many problems have been resolved that now I have even forgotten some of them. Getting back to my memoirs, and focusing on the aspect of my professional growth...

We became American Citizens in 1990. It seemed the correct thing to do. Life was not perfect, and never would be. We had been here six years and we had benefited from our move away from our island home. Our children were doing fairly well and we were coping better here in the United States than in our native land. It was something that we gave priority as early as possible. Ironically, again, my husband's citizenship papers came first and through some blunder from the Postal Service, my documents were lost. Consequently, we became citizens individually, on different dates, but by the end of 1990 the process was complete and we were officially naturalized citizens.

While all this was happening, another aspect of my life was changing. I applied to Loyola University to be a part of their nursing program that enabled Diploma nurses to work towards their Batchelor of Science in Nursing (BSN) degree. This was one of my goals. The VAMC (Veterans Affairs Medical Center), I later learned, would reimburse some of the tuition fees. I took out student loans to cover my expenses, because Loyola's tuition fees were a lot higher than those of the state college were. The nursing program at the state college was inflexible for me to work with. Loyola also had a diverse international student population and that appealed to me.

At Loyola, there were evening and weekend classes and somehow, I successfully worked through that program. Many nights I would leave work at seven pm, the end of my shift and drive to a six thirty or seven pm class. On the other hand, I would finish work at seven am and go to a nine am class. In advance, I would also plead with the faculty member giving the class and explain…

'I have registered for your course, I have to work twelve hour shifts and I will be late. I am unable to change my work schedule, and I fully intend to pass your course, so please have some patience with me when I arrive late'.

Loyola persevered and I graduated from that program in December 1993. A crisis and or my husband's temper tantrums seemed to occur coincidentally with many of my exams and sometimes I literally felt as if I was losing my mind.

Looking back, getting my BSN was really an anticlimax. I had been nursing for twenty-four years and so it enabled me to feel good that at last I had completed a degree program. It made me realize that I needed to go to graduate school in order to advance professionally. The children were thrilled at my graduation and I do believe that we both helped each other. I showed them that, at my age, returning to school was possible. They learned that it was easier to tackle ones dreams early in life, and that studying is a lot easier then, than waiting and trying to do it with a family. They learned first hand, that it was possible, but a lot more difficult.

In 1994, my daughter graduated from high school and started at Loyola University, in their Honor's program. She appeared to glide easily through the courses and she made friends easily. She had a good sense of humor and seemed to take life lightly. It took a lot of adjusting on my part to see my younger child as a capable adult. She realized that things were different with her brother away and she seemed to slide into the new role as a capable adult. She showed an excellent ability to organize people and things. She also made it clear to me and her father that she wanted no part of our family quarrels… she was tired of our constant bickering. She also made it clear that I should not continue in an obviously abusive marriage. She loved her father, but she did not like what we were doing to each other. As usual, at these times, I felt like a child. I knew what needed to be done, but I was not ready to take on that task. Years later, she revealed to me that she sought counseling on campus in order to be able to cope with problems at home. I shudder now thinking how this affected my children, and how I continued in a relationship and existed sometimes, in a state of mental lethargy…existing on a daily basis and not stopping to resolve this major dysfunction. At one point, I sought legal advice on divorce, and the male lawyer told me frankly, in a condescending tone...

'You cannot be living in the same house with your husband and file for divorce; you first have to move out'.

I was dumbfounded, because although the home was bought in both our names, I paid the mortgage. I caught a glimpse of how awkward this could be and I did not know how to begin to tackle this problem. I certainly could not move out nor did I want to. I was afraid of the consequences if I asked my husband to leave.

Now sometimes we humans view life from one angle, for which some things seem impossible. What I did not know was that the good Lord had planned a very convoluted way to relieve me of this home ownership and He introduced me to resourceful people who enabled me to view things differently. My problems continued but my coping mechanism changed.

My adult children, Maurice, a medical intern and Ann on the day of her graduation from Loyola University in New Orleans, and my parents in 1998.

My adult children: at Ann's graduation from law school in 2001.

MORE STUFF

Today people want and expect instant gratification. They expect immediate answers. However, before I start blaming this behavior on generations after me, I need to be honest. Instant gratification seems to be just simple human expectation; I also remember as a teenager, whenever I expressed my impatience with any process, my mother would say…

'Have patience' or…'Pray about it'.

I would snap back…usually out of earshot…

'And receive what is left over'.

Now I watch my own children conform with age, as they also realize that some things do take time to materialize. It took patience to resolve my future legal problems and that led me to more information that I would later use to my advantage.

In 1995, many of the houses in our subdivision were going into foreclosure. This was not good for the remaining homeowners, as home values were decreasing. It was time to leave that location and so it was time for me to sell that home. There was some equity over the eight years of ownership, otherwise it would have been more difficult to sell at that time. Now buying real estate was one experience for me, but selling was entirely different. It meant that I would be giving up my secure home, at a time when the market was not favorable to the seller, and I would be trying to find another place in a better location. Would I be able to afford to make this move? That was my silent fear. My children, who historically played an active role in any new family ventures, were unable to get involved as I would have liked. In all fairness, it was my responsibility to do this sale and it would have been unfair to expect them to give me their undivided attention. They were adults on campus, dealing with their own 'issues'. After all, I was the parent.

I contacted a female realtor from a very well established real estate company. I had only seen her name on a post card that was sent to me as an advertisement. She seemed to be confident and her sales record was impressive, so I signed a contract for her to sell the house. She also suggested, and I agreed, that the sale should include 'loan assumption' as an option. I did not know what that meant and when it was explained to me, I agreed. In retrospect, this is a good way to get real estate sold, if the buyer, the person assuming the loan, is honest and accepts the responsibility of assuming the debt. However, it is a passport for a dishonest person to acquire property, be delinquent, and be unaccountable for the debt, because it is the seller's name that remains on the documents, until the complete repayment of the loan.

The person who assumed my loan was dishonest. Also the sale did not go well at all. About two weeks after the closing, I was advised by the buyer's lawyer that all of the papers were not signed. When I complained to the real estate agent, she advised me to hire a lawyer. She suggested the lawyers used by her company. When I spoke to them they said, something like this had never happened before, and that they would be willing to give me legal advice. Personally, I did not trust them.

The fact is that the realtor had received her sale commission and I did not feel that I had a commitment from her. I called a lawyer from my church, who happened to teach my Sunday School class and she recommended a real estate lawyer whom she knew. We (my husband and I) spoke with him and he scrutinized the documents and set up the process to have the error corrected. What I did not know until five years after, is that, he suspected that there would be future problems; and I did, a few months before the statute of limitations expired.

In addition to that problem, the buyer made only a few regular payments on the loan. I was made aware of this by the mortgage company and eventually the home that I 'sold' went into foreclosure. By this time, I had bought a second home. I was unable to pay two mortgages. It would be an understatement to say that there were a lot of problems.

The lawyer told me not to worry about it and that he would 'sort this out.' He was very reassuring, and I had my doubts. I worried incessantly! Even when I felt that I had knelt down and prayed and handed it over to God, and should have forgotten about it, subconsciously, I still fretted. To top it all, the buyer filed a lawsuit against us for selling her property that was not 'safe'. Since assuming the loan, the house was burgled. Of course, she filed a claim with, and was paid by her insurance company. It was all happening. When I felt that it was all just too much, the lawyer called me one day at work and said that he had some good news for me…everything was resolved, our names were 'cleared' and even the pending lawsuit was dismissed. I was elated! Only then did I realize exactly how stressful the entire process had been and it was literally as if a load was removed from my shoulder.

What worked in my favor, as a result, of all that legal experience, was that I purchased the second home in my name only. Louisiana is a 'community property' state, but I learnt that the spouse could sign a form of 'non-intervention' (or a similar term), relinquishing his/her right to ownership. My husband agreed to sign that form and again, he made no contribution to the deposit. We remained in this house for eleven years until it was sold after Katrina.

That home became the sanctuary for my daughter and any of her friends who were homesick and needed a home cooked meal, and for my son and any of his friends who simply needed a break from the rigors of their Medical Internship and residency programs. While we were living there our son graduated from Medical School and our daughter from Law School, and I managed to get my M.Ed., and last, but not least, my husband graduated with a degree in Accounting.

From a marriage perspective, our dysfunction continued. Our movements through the house were carefully orchestrated to avoid each other. During company we coped by pretending that we lived as a united front. When company was absent, I would get home and eat dinner, watch the news in time to be in bed shortly before my husband came in. Sometimes we hardly spoke to each other. I tried to avoid a confrontation, and remained silent most of the time. He watched television and there was no room for conversation. On one of my sister's visits to New Orleans, she remarked, plainly, as usual,

'You have bought and live in such a beautiful home, but you are not enjoying it…you are only living in it'.

I thought about what she said. Somehow, my sister has always been able to recognize when something was not right; this time was no exception.

I had already moved out of the master bedroom, it was not a healthy arrangement, it was strained and I simply did not have the energy to change any of it.

JUST ANOTHER WORKING DAY

It was another regular, busy day at work. The usual meetings were over. It was afternoon. My hours of work were 8:00am to 4:30pm. As usual, something would need resolving at the last minute and leaving at 4:30pm would be unusual. I got another buzz on my pager to call the operator and so I did. I heard the voice of my Internist's nurse saying that he wanted to talk with me about my recent chest x-ray. Automatically I listened...

'Kathleen there are some abnormalities here...enlarged Lymph nodes, I am not sure what this means...fortunately, there are no fluid levels that we can detect on this film...I can recommend a Cardiothoracic surgeon...who may want to do biopsy'.

I heard his voice, I did not listen to all of what he was saying, he lost me at..."enlarged lymph nodes" and I woke up at "cardiothoracic surgeon". My first reaction was...why is my doctor telling me about the chest x-ray results of a veteran? My mind went amok and in many directions. I had to disengage myself from the role of "health professional" to that of "patient". All I remember saying was,

'Let me share this with my son, and I will call you back.'

'Sure' said my doctor, 'have him call me anytime...here is another contact number'.

I had built up a good rapport with my Internist over the years. He knew my husband and he knew that our children were away from home. I admired how he shared information and then found time to talk and answer any questions that needed to be answered. So I know that this needed attention. I was wide awake now. I shared the news with my son, who said

'Yes. You need to have that biopsy done ASAP'.

It is always easy to give harsh advice, but following it will always be an age old problem! My dear boss, the Chief of Surgery, agreed with all that was said, he reassured me as I shared my medical history with him…that it was a simple procedure. I knew that…but it was major for the patient…ME.

I played with whether or not I should share this news with my parents… they were so far away and I know that they would really be worried for me. I decided to tell them. My mother was surprisingly re-assuring; she remained a woman of strong faith and reassured me that she would pray that I would be all right and that no further intervention would be necessary. She asked me twice if I had told her everything… probably she suspected that I was trying to protect her. I was surprised at her response and that really gave my soul extra courage.

I had planned taking my vacation to visit my sister and we planned a wonderful holiday. If I had to have further surgery, my first reaction was…my holiday would have to be cancelled. Talk about getting ones priorities right! I had to re-focus…this was my health…vacations could always be postponed.

Well the biopsy would be done as an outpatient procedure. I could not drive home and I would need someone to be there with me afterwards. This was not news to me…this is the advise that I pass on to our patients everyday. I told my husband and he promised to take me to the hospital and take me home. I also shared the news with my very good friend at work. I needed to ensure that someone would be there for me when I woke up from the anesthetic. I needed someone, beside the regular surgery staff at that hospital, who could identify if I was in distress and alert the medical staff. Silently and probably selfishly, I decided that seeing a familiar face on awakening would reassure me, in my stupor, that I was alive.

During my pre-op interview with the Anesthetist, I asked him to be careful with my dental work and to place the endotracheal tube away from my recent bridge work. I also shared with him the fact that I felt that I had arthritic changes in my neck, so I asked him to note this on my exam, because I know that my neck would be extended during surgery and I feared that I could be at risk , and end up with skeletal problems. He reassured me that they would be careful. He may have felt that I was too involved, but silently we both knew that nurses and doctors make the worst patients. He had a wonderful bedside manner.

I got to the hospital early and I waited patiently for my name to be called. Conversation at this point was impossible, I wanted to be calm, I wanted to silently meditate. I had to reassure myself that I was coping. Both my children were away, miles away, I am not sure that my daughter was coping well with this news. My friend from work promised me that she would be there when I came out of surgery, and that enabled me to relax.

My husband decided that instead of waiting with me, he could go and get 'some chores done', and he left. There were delays, as some cases were taking longer than planned. During this time an elderly lady came into the waiting room and sat across from me. She seemed agitated and I asked if she was all right. She gave a simple explanation for her mood and soon her company came and reassured her.

I sat alone and I was on the brink of tears…at this moment I wanted to have someone beside me, it would have been comforting. The reality was, I told myself…you came into this world alone…and you will die alone. If this was my day to die…there was nothing that I could do about it. I could not do the surgery, I could not administer the anesthetic…I would humbly submit my body to the experts and pray for success. I felt like a tiny speck, about the size of a grain of sand, as the world's activities continued unsuspectingly, while I faced my surgery.

STUPID PRAYER

There have been a few times when I have looked back at something that I did and wondered,

"What was I thinking?'

Have you ever had the opportunity to be in a situation that you could get anything that you asked for? I remember as adults my sister asked me...

'If you had an audience with God, and He told you that you could have one wish granted in your lifetime...what would you wish for sis?'

I did not hesitate, immediately I said ...

'World peace'.

I probably sounded like some new beauty contestant, but that is what I felt was the biggest problem preventing humans from peacefully co-habiting the universe; and who else could resolve it in an instant, but the one who created it all? My sister looked at me as if I had answered her in a foreign language and said...

'World peace eh? Would you really? That is interesting.'

I got the feeling that once again I did not give the correct answer.

I will 'fast forward' my thoughts to the year 2000, the new millennium. When I was told that my chest x-ray was abnormal...the diagnosis could be narrowed down to Lymphoma or Sarcoidosis. I was afraid of what the biopsy would confirm. As a person who believed in the power of prayer, I turned to the church family to seek their prayers. I honestly believe that if more voices could pray on my behalf, a greater impact could be made on presenting my plight to God. It was not easy to pray and carry on with my life...I worried continuously. None of what was happening managed to convince me that my life was over. I honestly felt physically and mentally tired and I looked forward to my vacation time when I had planned going away and having a good time away from all my stressors. This event somehow riveted me to take stock of myself. It forced me to pay attention and to get all the necessary assistance that was available, and to work hard at resolving this crisis. To me it was a crisis.

Well hearing that it was narrowed down to two conditions, I thought with my simple human mind, that I had to choose which one I could cope with, the dumbest thing that I did in my life was to pray to God that I had Sarcoidosis…I figured that I could cope with that diagnosis better than Lymphoma. It never dawned on me that I was praying to the Superior being who is able to do anything, and who could even let the Lymph nodes subside and let the entire scare disappear. I prayed for Sarcoidosis…and when I awoke from the anesthetic…I heard my friend's voice saying…

'Kathleen…they confirmed that it is Sarcoidosis'…

'Thank God' I said…'now I can still go on my holiday.'

Looking back, that was another of the dumbest things that I have done in my life …that I am able to share with the sane world.

There is no cure for Sarcoidosis. The cause of this disease is unknown. This is a condition characterized by widespread tiny granulomatous lesions that may affect any organ or tissue of the body. In my case, it affected my thoracic cavity. There are many theories as to what seems to cause it, but to date, none have been proven. That is what I prayed for. Realizing my blunder, I just prayed to God to enable me to cope with all that was happening and I also prayed for my survival.

I went on my holiday, my flight was a couple days after my biopsy and off I went with my dressing intact, and I had a wonderful time. On return I started to feel some obstruction in my throat on swallowing and I was sure that I was dealing with some internal suture that had not dissolved. The kind surgeon explained that my symptoms were connected to my condition, as he felt sure that the suture had already dissolved.

I was referred to a Pulmonologist who would now be responsible for my care. It was love at first sight. He proved to be a wonderful person and many days I dragged myself to his office from work. I would be re-assured that there were many different stages of this disease and that sometimes it goes into remission. The nurse for this unit was a very pretty, very pleasant, very positive personality, and I had a difficult time relating to what advice she gave me… all her statements had hope. I sometimes looked around at the other patients in the waiting room and my thoughts would indeed drift to pray that I would not progress to the advanced end stage. At those moments I simply prayed that I would be allowed to live one day at a time and to be able to cope with anything. Sometimes, I even thought begrudgingly of the nurse…

'It is easy for you to give me advise, you are not ill'.

Slowly, mentally, I moved away from that mode of thinking and I coped with life as it was presented to me…one day at a time. For my own peace of mind I saw an Allergist who confirmed that what I had was not due to allergies. My Pathology slides were reviewed at another facility and second opinion confirmed the first diagnosis. My sister-in–law told me that she was similarly diagnosed several years ago and that she had been under the care of a Naturalist, and she had good results. I went to see him, and I was put on a diet that excluded yeast and most gluten. All my favorite fruits and cheeses and alcoholic beverages were forbidden and so were processed foods. I was told that it would take time for my body to adjust to the changes and that I should be patient. Mine adjusted almost the next day. I really felt better.

My condition progressed rapidly through to the third stage and my chest x-rays did not look good at all. Coping took patience and hope. On one visit I was told that the common treatment is Steroids, and that I should give this suggestion some thought because I may have to start taking this medication. I attended support group meetings. I did not enjoy sitting with a group that discussed their illness, and sometimes it felt as if some tried to focus on how much worse off their stage was, and how no medication seemed to help. Sometimes I thought the focus was more on the symptoms and not on the relief of symptoms. When I mentioned that I started this diet that worked for me…someone said…

'I am not that sick that I cannot eat everything'.

My status remained at stage three, and I continued with lifestyle changes. I was acutely aware of dust and smoke and tried to create a clean home environment. So far, I was not on steroids.

After three years, I went for my usual follow up visit and as usual, I had my Pulmonary Function tests and chest x-rays before seeing the doctor. Great! They could not find my x-ray, I had to wait longer than planned…here I was undressed and waiting in the exam room hearing the footsteps rushing into every room but mine…OK …I would wait, after all the x-ray was taken on site…how could it be lost? I consoled myself. Now my blood pressure would register above normal and that would present more thoughts that something else was probably wrong. There were voices outside my room; my doctor was calling to his colleague…

'Look at this.' He was saying. I listened curiously; did they find my film? Were they talking about some new development? I could not bear it anymore; I left the room and asked them …

'Is that mine guys?' Well they brought the film into my room and showed me the results. I looked at it and my first reaction was…now they have the dam wrong film! So I got up and checked the name and the date…hey, mistakes do happen! I was the patient! I needed to convince myself that at least it was the correct film! It was!

My Pulmonologist said…

'Your chest x-ray is almost normal, Kathleen'

...something is working! I had been praying for this moment for the last three years and when it did come true ...my first reaction was to doubt it! I displayed another human characteristic.

I was told that I could be in remission, if there were no worse developments for five years. Now I was ecstatic! I thanked God for His role in this and asked that my doubt be forgiven and I made a pledge to live. I felt as if I had been shown a work of art on which a new, bright light was focused. I could now see it clearly and appreciate the hidden beauty of the colors. I could also appreciate the time and patience that it must have taken the artist to complete His masterpiece.

SELF-ASSESSMENT AND REFINANCING

Periodically I spend some of my time on self-assessment and post Sarcoidosis was a good time for a re-assessment of my life. I tend to look back at what I have done; I do a quick evaluation to decide what worked for or against me. If I can make changes, I do so and then I move forward with my life. That decision is usually final. I really dislike having to return to visit former jobsites or even driving past former residences. Once I make that decision, I try not to regret it.

I started seriously thinking of retirement and tried to make a decision as to when it could be possible. What I found out, or the reality of what I had to face, was that I could not retire before age 62 and that I needed to work seriously at removing my debt and planning towards accumulating a projected total for my future. It was possible. I had fallen victim to debt from being the typical working mother, the single household support person. I charged air travel home from college for the children, supplemented health insurance premiums for the children as they outgrew my family plan, paid large, unaffordable dental fees, supplemented their off campus accommodation, and paid for my graduate education. I also tried a brief period as a rental property owner. That, along with trying to repair rental property, accounted for a drastic increase in my debt. One moment I was coping well paying my bills on time and in what seemed like a 'heartbeat', every cent of my salary was just barely repaying bills. It was frightening and sometimes I felt very helpless.

My solution was to borrow from myself. I tackled well-needed home improvement repairs, I destroyed all except one of my credit cards, I refinanced my home and my car loans and I sold the rental property. Ironically selling the rental property was the easiest sale I had done, and the one that I feared would have been the most awkward. The buyer actually came to me and it was a cash transaction. I thought the worse of him at our first meeting, and immediately I thought that he was a drug dealer and that I should stay clear of him. He turned out to be a very ambitious investor who was busy acquiring old houses, refurbishing and reselling them. To me, it was the easiest sale that I ever transacted.

With all my plans to retire, what I did not know is that my husband was also monitoring my savings and he calculated my retirement fund. I was married to a crazy man but he was no fool. Again, it showed that the best plan can be rendered worthless by a simple oversight. It was slowly dawning on me although I did not know how I was going to get out of my marriage, that remaining would not be a healthy choice. My lifelong teaching was always to buy what you can afford, and so to be in a situation where I owed a lot of money made me feel as if I had failed to live by those basic principles. It was a relief to be able to plan a solution to this problem.

It felt good to be working and paying off my debts. Realizing that I was able to remove that burden from my shoulders and that I would be able to afford to leave my employment while I was still able to enjoy my life with my five senses and my skeletal frame intact, was additional relief and motivation. Many of my colleagues were not that fortunate and several ended up with back or some joint malfunction that forced them into 'retirement' prematurely.

Here I was making plans to retire, and trying to be fiscally responsible. My husband on the other hand, did not seem to change. His debts remained 'in limbo'. At one point he even stated that he might have to declare bankruptcy. I was distraught. This would certainly be to my disadvantage especially as I was busy filing papers with immigration and making plans for my parents to live with us. He knew where my panic buttons were located and he knew when to press them. This time however, I continued with my plans. I would repay my debt! I did not even consider tackling his. That was his responsibility. It took me about four years to accomplish my task and the best news came with a notice of my last payment.

I could now only concern myself with praying for physical health and diligently saving for my retirement. I accepted that life has many obstacles, but daily I realized that solutions do exist and many times it is up to the individual to find those solutions or to have a good idea of what they should be. There is no one out there, except God, I have found, who knows better than yourself what will work best for you. So I prodded on, unsuspecting that August 2005 had more surprises and more unpredictable changes in store for us.

POST SARCOIDOSIS

Well…I decided to live my life, to enjoy each day fully, to relieve some of the stressors in my life. We, my sister and I, had already decided that our parents would reside with me. This entailed completing numerous forms for Immigration authorities, having physical exams, my providing proof that I could support them here in this country; and their disposing of their possessions and deciding what was really worth taking. It was difficult, but my father was a very practical minded person and so he made some good decisions and saved us all a lot of time and hurt emotions.

During 2001 and 2005, I can remember ringing in the New Year on the Las Vegas strip, a truly wonderful, breathtaking experience. I must admit that I like Las Vegas. I am no gambler, but the city has an interesting history and the bold extravagance, and neon lights, to me are mesmerizing. We always got $20.00 in nickels each, and when we spent that…our gambling splurge ended. I think that it would be easier for me to burn some notes than to lose money at a casino. As I do not see myself burning any notes, I know that I will not be tempted to splurge beyond my grand total of $20.00.

I also remember on another trip to Las Vegas, with 'my partner in crime', my sister, we had one of the best holidays; this time we accidentally heard a Reggae Band playing in one of the hotels that we were passing through on the way to our hotel. Well, we 'old broads' could not ignore that sound. Our feet followed our ears to the music, met the leader, who admitted that this was only an experiment for them, but in an environment far from the Caribbean,

'Nobody would know the difference.'

My sister and I convinced ourselves that we would not stay too late at this spot, and that we would watch the time closely, as our flight out the next morning was at 7:00 am, and we had an early shuttle to catch. Boy! Subconsciously, we just threw caution through the window! With some Myers

Rum and that pulsating, contagious music from home, we danced and had so much fun! At one point we even, well my sister, even demonstrated the precise movement for some lyrics. The short version to that story is that we got back to our hotel in time to pack, have some coffee and meet the shuttle. We kept saying to each other…

'How did that happen? We cannot do without sleep at our age. What were we thinking?'…

The flight back home was empty and the flight attendant mentioned that we could be more comfortable, by spreading out the seating arrangement more; we were so depleted that we huddled together fast asleep, as other passengers spread out and made themselves comfortable. We had no more energy to move even an inch once we settled into our seats.

On trips home to work with our parents, sometimes we would arrange to be there together and then try to enjoy just the simple beauty of nature as it surrounded us with familiar flowers, in full bloom, or the tropical fruits in abundance and the natural cuisine. At first, we tried to meet up with other family members, but over the years people just seemed to be totally engrossed in their own affairs and never seemed to have time to visit or to return phone calls. Some family or friends, whom we met up with, always seemed to make an effort at impressing us as to how well they were doing…a factor that I still find very boring. My sister and I as adults who had been surviving independently for many years decided in the future not to contact any friends or family on subsequent trips home. We just had wonderful visits. Very busy, but very relaxing, in a strange sense and I got the opportunity to put on 'hold' any work, health or marital issues and just immerse myself in what was happening to our parents at that time.

On one visit home, the last time that I accepted my elderly father's offer to collect me from the airport, I completely lost 'my cool'. Driving in Jamaica is crazy…frequently drivers ignore road signs, not to mention traffic lights. At busy intersections, it is not unusual to observe traffic 'creeping forward' slowly, against the red lights, because the drivers say convincingly…

'The light is not working'.

Well my father was driving home from the airport and, for the first time I was acutely aware that he had a problem with his peripheral vision. He merrily veered to the extreme right or left at inappropriate times while other drivers openly swore at him. My embarrassing moment came as we got to a busy intersection and after hesitating, my father continued across two lanes of traffic approaching my side. I felt sure that the cars would collide, I repeatedly pressed my imaginary brake pedal, and when that failed to have any effect, I heard my mouth utter distinctly a very unladylike local expletive.

It all happened very quickly and my father's eyes reflected surprise, shame and amusement. He said coolly...

'So your brakes did not work Miss Kaths?'

During this period of my life that my sister and I pledged to travel together, we spent time on the south coast of Spain, Gibraltar, visited Belgium, France and of course saw more of England. I appreciated how lucky I was, first to be alive, second to be able to travel and third to have a good travel partner in my sister. We could almost read each others' minds when we saw something that was funny, and sometimes we would deliberately avoid eye contact with each other, to prevent a spontaneous embarrassing laugh. It was a wonderful time.

On one occasion, during a double-decked bus tour of Paris, we sat upstairs of course to get the full view of the city. It was cold and got colder as the day progressed. The upper deck of the bus was open. I was distracted and when I caught sight of my sister beside me; she had metamorphosized into some Middle Eastern ancestor, complete with burka. She knew that I would lose my composure in the midst of all those strangers and she looked at me intently with very piercing eyes. That is all that was visible from her neck up....her eyes! She held me in fierce eye contact as I simply exploded...to hell with the company, this woman beside me was warm and crazy. She had wrapped and draped a beautiful scarf into a style the designer could never have imagined. Today's vocabulary would describe it as 'wardrobe malfunction!' Together we laughed hysterically as I asked this person beside me...

'Have you seen my sister?'

Enjoying a good joke with my sister, in Nevada, in 2001.

At the Esplanade Mall in New Orleans in 2000, with my sister and my daughter.

KATRINA AND ME

Before writing about hurricane Katrina, I have to share my childhood hurricane experience because again it enabled me to make what proved to be a wise decision.

It was August 1951 and I was a small child in the country. We were visiting our grandmother in the city. I do remember that our visit was shortened as we heard on the news that hurricane Charlie was approaching our island and should 'make landfall' that night. Looking back now, I wonder if the adults thought that maybe the hurricane would change its course, because we were miles away from home. We should not have been in the city. The Eastern side of the island would be affected and it was expected to be severe. So, we said our goodbyes and headed to the bus terminal (station) to return to our home.

We heard our mother talk with the bus driver, she was worried that probably we would not get home safely…he reassured her that we would all be fine. At that time there was bright sunshine and no sign of rain. He also reminded my mother that the rains would start later that day but we would be home before the weather changed. His prediction was accurate.

We arrived home early that day and observed everyone scurrying to nail boards over the windows of our home, collect containers of water for drinking and for hygiene purposes and refilling the larder with extra supplies. We saw our father come home for brief moments to ensure that preparations were going as planned and my sister and I watched in awe, not knowing what to expect. They told us that there would be heavy rain and strong winds and we should not stay near the windows. The heavy rain started and we were settled in bed. We could see that my mother was worried; and my father kept coming and going as he went out with men carrying lanterns to access crop damage and to make sure that people in the vicinity were safe. I remember his returning before the wind started and, as children, we felt that we would be secure because our tall and strong hero was there to protect us.

The storm came as predicted. The windows literally shook and we could hear the heavy rain pounding on the roof. Sleep was not an option. We were frightened. I thought that the shear force of wind and rain would probably split our home into pieces. We huddled with our parents in one end of the house as my mother prayed loudly, asking God to protect us all. She sometimes chanted like a 'mantra'

'Lord have mercy, Christ have mercy'.

That night certainly seemed to last forever in my memory. The next morning we heard of the severe damage that was done to acres of crops and of homes that were destroyed, people who were made homeless, we saw the damage to the roof of our home and heard of roads that were impassable. We also heard of severe damage that was done to homes in Kingston, as news came through on more areas that were affected.

I was a child and it was difficult to understand how long recovery from that hurricane took. I do remember the dreaded fear that I experienced, of the quick bus ride home and the awful sound of the wind against the windows of our home and the dreaded sound of windows shaking against that force. I do remember the sound of the wind and rain pounding on the roof, and the bare appearance of acres of land previously filled with flourishing green fields of bananas and sugar cane. Those images have been encrypted in my mind. I was only six years old.

Fate led me to the United States and eventually to New Orleans. I previously knew very little of this city but over the 20 years that I lived there I grew to enjoy the Big Easy. I certainly learnt to appreciate its cuisine and jazz music, to quickly name a few things that I truly loved. Preparing for annual hurricane seasons was not new to my family, as we had to do this while in Jamaica. In New Orleans our family had an emergency kit with canned foods and first-aid supplies. We actually had to evacuate on two previous occasions in the twenty years, but because I was a part of the emergency team, my family was allowed to stay at the hospital while I worked. In 2003 or 2004 we actually left town and drove to the north of the state. I did not realize that this would be a rehearsal. The public television station did a series on our city preparing for a hurricane and showed the predicted city damage that would ensue from different categories of hurricanes. My emergency kit expanded to include large sheets of plastic, strong rope, some basic tools and I made a mental note that I needed an axe, in case we were trapped in the attic of our home.

The hurricane season started in 2005 and as usual, I tracked the course of any threats on my computer and would decide for myself what section of the

Gulf coast would be the likely target. Hurricane Katrina was no exception. I took a keen interest as it headed for Florida but changed its course and could probably hit New Orleans directly. The prediction of a 'Bull's Eye' hit from a category five hurricane was not good news.

Previously I remained home and experienced weather that produced winds 75 -90 miles an hour. I was frightened. Our home nestled under five enormous, old Live Oak trees that were trimmed regularly, leaving at least six feet of clear space away from our roof. Those huge branches, scratched, scraped and swayed in all directions during that night as the wind acted like the conductor of nature's orchestra. I realized that staying home was a grave error and that if the weather conditions deteriorated then, evacuation would have been impossible.

Before the pending hurricane, my personal plans for August 2005 included meeting my son and sister in Sussex, England doing more sightseeing, enjoying each other's company, and then traveling to Italy, with my sister, for a wonderful holiday.

News of the hurricane's path did not sound good for the city of New Orleans…the number Category 5 stuck in my mind. Mentally, I could see clearly the vivid simulated photographs from that television program showing potential damage and flooding to areas of the city. It looked grave. I decided that I would evacuate and shared this thought with my husband, who was undecided. Fortunately, the weekend was approaching and I planned on instinct. I would travel east on the 1-10, cross over the narrowest point of Lake Pontchartrain and drive North out of the city to Alexandria. I decided that evacuation had to be to an area away from water and the approaching wind.

Mentally, planning what I should take on this trip was difficult. As a naturalized citizen of this country, our citizenship papers and passports, headed the list, drivers license, social security cards, the children's college certificates, insurance papers, bank information and cards, my professional licensing information were included. I packed clothes for a four day weekend. My suitcase for holiday travel was already packed and that was thrown in the trunk of the car. It was partially organized. We would evacuate, be delayed …the worse case scenario…until Wednesday the latest. I would drive back directly to the airport, catch my flight and continue with my vacation, as planned.

City officials were planning to make a public announcement on mandatory evacuation the Saturday morning and to update citizens on the hurricane status. I decided to leave long before this. If we were going to be told to evacuate…then because of our location on the city's West Bank, we would probably not be included in the first group of evacuees and our access to the nearest bridge leading to, and out of the city, would be blocked. My husband was reluctant to leave, his car would be left behind, maybe I was taking this too seriously and worrying unnecessarily, maybe we should wait.

I packed my car…gave him time to pack some belongings, decided not even to move 'things' to the second floor, concentrate on keeping vital documentation for our survival and identification and drive to safety.

My car 'Trippy,' a Dodge Intrepid, was ready for the adventure. He glided out of the driveway…I silently prayed to Jesus…

'Please take us safely out of the city and please guide us through the unknown, help us to find somewhere to sleep…walk with us on our journey'.

It sounded eerily similar to our prayer in 1984, when we left our home and family in Kingston to start a new life in Arkansas.

The morning was clear and sunny and the skies were blue. There was very little traffic for the duration of our trip. I drove with determination. I did not tell my neighbors. They had lived in their home for years and even experienced a previously severe hurricane and they survived. We arrived in Alexandria and quickly found a hotel room for that night. I was reassured that it would be no problem to extend our stay, if that was necessary. We walked around the city and did nothing special…except listened to developments in New Orleans.

EPISODE TWO...KATRINA

We did not plan on staying more than the weekend at this hotel. We really did not have the funds to be able to afford more than a long weekend. We were the average family...our children were out of college, we were now at the empty nest syndrome stage...the home was recently re-financed for a better interest rate...we were trying to remain out of frivolous credit card debt. The desk clerk at the hotel could not definitely promise us that we could remain in the room, but hinted that it maybe OK. On Sunday morning, we were told that we would have to vacate our room as it was booked by people from Florida. Then we soon realized that the norm for some families is to book rooms in hotels far away from the course of the hurricane, and stay there until the threat is over.

Well we left the hotel early and we were referred to a nearby church that was an evacuation center...they had no room. We were referred to other centers in town...and could find no rooms. Then someone gave us an address of a center nearby. When we got there it was literally a camp site. After registering at the office on site, we were taken on a tour. People who used this area regularly were arriving, cleaning down bunk beds with bleach solutions and making up beds with bed linen that they had brought. There was a shower, unisex, with a cloth curtain approximately eighteen inches from the floor. My roaming eyes could definitely decipher male from female feet. My concerns with this site were many. It was in an open field. We parked our cars on the grass that was not a good plan with the predicted bad weather. The unisex showers provided minimal privacy...the sleeping areas were also shared. I was very selfish, I saw the following vision. It would rain very heavily, the grass would be inundated with water, my car would be stuck, and I would have to sleep with my belongings under my head while my husband and I would be trying to fight to protect my honor. My husband would definitely get into some conflict with someone...he is not a 'people person'. Above all, I would not even be able to get to my car and if I did, the field would be flooded and driving would be impossible.

So we said goodbye to that place and drove further north. I had no GPS, but I did have a road map. My husband said cheerily…

'We could go back to Arkansas'.

I really felt relieved when I left Arkansas. We both did, and to be honest, I wanted to be as far as possible from there. Resolutely I decided that I would go to the border of Louisiana, and even drive around Arkansas, but I would not go back to that state.

At this point, you all may have guessed that our marriage was strained. My husband and I were barely coping, but the up-coming hurricane had us preoccupied with our safety and conversation, at this stage, flowed amicably without friction.

The drive further north was tedious. We were both tired, and we got used to seeing the same cars ahead or behind us. We were not on the interstate and we stopped at every motel that was visible. We got the same response…

'No rooms are available'.

I felt tired. I wanted to stop anywhere, the prospect of a room and a bed to sleep on seemed distant. The more we drove on the more we seemed to be driving in a convoy. I remember passing a hospital and decided…

'Push comes to shove' I would park in the parking lot and we could at least sleep for the night. The journey continued. Then we saw a Motel 8 sign, it was not on the main road, and I had passed it. I turned around and finally found it. I wearily left the car…it was my turn to go in…and so I entered and asked in a very exasperated tone…

'Do you have any rooms available?'

The clerk said 'yes, but you may not want it, it is for the handicapped'.

My face lit up, I was overjoyed!

'I'll take it',

I heard myself saying. We booked for two nights, to be honest I was not even sure what town we were in and I really did not care…we had found a bed! Well it was dark and I did not care where we were, slowly we unloaded our belongings from the car. The car could be stolen and it would be a shame to lose our papers and clothes also, in the event of that actually happening. There was a TV and microwave oven in the room and it seemed very, very small, but tonight, it was paradise.

We listened to the news on CNN, Katrina was advancing, it was slightly downgraded and it was heading for New Orleans, our home. We prayed for the safety of our city, for our safety, we prayed for our sins to be forgiven and for us to be able to cope with the outcome and we slept.

Early the next morning, I awoke to the CNN news. I saw scenes of New Orleans and the French Quarter; they had survived the hurricane!

'Thank God' I said aloud.

I watched views of a few people walking in the French Quarter, with drinks in hand; they were obviously trying to re-group with friends and neighbors. The interesting thing about writing about this is that I find that I am unable to give an accurate sequence of events. I do wonder if my memory would be better if I had remained in the city. I am not sure.

At some point during the news, I do remember hearing the voice of a caller saying,

'If the storm is over, then can someone tell me why the water level is rising in my yard?'

Like helpless robots, we continued to watch the news. I froze in my seat and felt nauseated and helpless. Further news confirmed what we thought. The Levees had broken!

'My God' I said finally, 'thousands will lose their lives!'

I do not remember for how much longer we watched the news, seeing the water level rise in the city, imagining what it was really like. I wept, I felt ill, alone, frightened and almost totally helpless, like an unidentified dot in the vast universe.

Gaining composure was slow, but I remember first ensuring the room for a week, and then I made a call to the insurance company. I was asked if I had a home in New Orleans, I said I am not sure …

'Do you think that you have lost anything?' the female voice said.

I remember saying, 'My dear, I may have lost everything'.

In one day, we realized that things had changed dramatically. I had cried enough and now my 'nursing mode and critical thinking' took over. I bought a 'pay as you go' phone and requested a number with an area code away from the affected areas. On this I emailed our son and daughter informing them of our location. I called FEMA and got our names and location on record. Soon immediate family was aware of our location, and the necessary authorities to assist had our names on file. I finally was able to speak to someone connected to my work and my name was on the list of staff that was safe.

It would be approximately two weeks before the roads into our section of the city were cleared to traffic and we ventured home. The scene was almost unrecognizable, homes were destroyed, communities were barren, cars were on their sides as if some huge finger simply flicked them to a new location. There was a distinct smell of death and decay. Slowly and silently we drove into the city and across the bridge to our home in Algiers. Many homes had blue tarp on their roofs and trailers were parked on lawns and in driveways. Finally we arrived home, our area was intact! The utilities were intact! Absent mindedly, I used the garage door opener and the door opened! Our large oak trees lost many branches that fitted around our home and beside the patio glass door like bubble wrap protecting a precious package. The fence was down, we had to pull away tree branches to get into the house…but it was intact. We both knelt down and cried and loudly thanked God for delivering us safely from nature's tragedy.

The next months were very busy. I thanked God that I was an employee with the Federal Government, because assistance came swiftly and comprehensively. I was deployed to another state to work, I got the opportunity to sell my home, put furniture in storage and relocate, and I got the opportunity to apply for work in other states. Thanks to efficient record keeping, my employee record was readily available. Thanks to an employing body that identified that we all suffered some post-traumatic symptoms, we were given the opportunity to receive counseling.

Together we moved from New Orleans in March 2006. Our home was sold, at a profit before we arrived at our new destination a five-hour drive away. I started working in Memphis, TN., and remained there for a year. The stress of the move, a shaky marriage and work finally took its toll one day and I went to Human Recourses to review my retirement information. I would be able to cope financially, if I was careful with the available funds that I had accumulated over the years. My peers were dying; their eyes reflected no emotion.

I decided to stop working, to give up the stressors, to move on and live. There was so much more that I wanted to do with the right side of my brain and it was about time that I started.

FOLLOWING KATRINA

My sister and I thanked God for the good health and long life that our elderly parents enjoyed. However we realized that it was not to their advantage to be left alone, although physically they were independent, our mother did have dementia and, typically, her short term memory was gone. They continued to have household help and so we were assured that the house was maintained. My father competently paid the bills and continued with his singing on the church choir and keeping in touch with a small group of friends and neighbors. He coped independently, but being elderly himself, coping with mom's care was very difficult.

My sister and I decided to visit frequently, in order to keep abreast of exactly how well they were coping. Ideally, it would have been best if we could have found a suitable, younger person to live at home with them, but that was not possible. Finally, my father surprisingly agreed to my offer for them to move to New Orleans and live with me and my husband. This was probably decided in 2003. We filed the necessary immigration papers, and allowed the long beaurocratic process to run its timely course.

For many years prior to this, my sister and I talked through many scenarios on care of our parents, in an attempt to find a practical solution. There were none. We were worried that in today's time and with a high crime rate in Kingston, they were vulnerable and we feared that they would become another crime victim 'statistic'. The neighbors and other people in the community knew them well, they respected and 'looked out for and protected' them well. However, it was the strangers we feared. With each visit home, we observed new people in the community and some were not very friendly. Their mannerisms demonstrated that they disapproved of my parents, and saw them as living too long and not serving any useful role in society. So when my father finally agreed to leave his home and come to live with us in New Orleans, I was thrilled.

In the midst of all this Katrina came and changed my life's routine. I was still determined however that my parents would relocate; that part of my plans would not be altered.

Getting through the application process for immigration included completing numerous forms, having physical exams, immunizations and interviews, to mention a few. Finally the application was successful in 2005 and a date was set for travel. My sister and I were very impressed with how competently our father disposed of their belongings, selling what he thought could be sold, and giving away some things to people whom he dearly cared for and who would find splendid use for their gifts. Finally a buyer was found for my parents' home and their travel date depended on how quickly my husband and I could find a permanent address.

Remember that during this time my husband and I moved to Mississippi, where I was deployed. We were provided accommodation in a small apartment. I remained professionally suspended trying to function in a similar role to the one in New Orleans and trying, against all odds, to complete a project that was unfinished because of Katrina. I found Mississippi depressing. I was surrounded by my peers at work, but we all moved together as a group, a sad group. We each dealt with our different stages of grief and individually, we made our own decisions on coping. Minute hindrances at work to me were seen as major obstacles and I cried very easily. During this time I also traveled back to New Orleans on week-ends to ensure that our home remained intact and that things there were in order. I also continued to travel to Jamaica to support my parents.

It is not surprising that I opted to accept counseling from a Psychologist and found the sessions helpful. I also need to add that my daughter had to remind me that therapy was available and that I should take it. I was always a very private person, keeping 'issues/problems' to myself. Surprisingly, I found that talking through my problems with a third person, who was a stranger, proved to be refreshing. I was finally taking time from work to admit that problems existed and, hopefully I would work to find resolutions.

However, I found myself talking more about my marriage and some difficulties that were emphasized since Katrina. My husband and I had drifted apart. The children were grown; they were independent and away from home. We seemed to argue over everything and there were many times when I found solace in avoiding conflicts and thus prevent having to argue and repeatedly try to give explanations to simple actions. I had been unhappy for years and I evaded admitting that I needed to break free. I did not know how to do this amicably and silently I felt guilty if a solution to the problem was to abandon my marriage.

There were multiple stressors occurring in my life simultaneously. I had to relocate because the floods from the hurricane had erased my job and inundated my home city. My parents were relocating and coming to live with me. My marriage was moving towards a crisis. Friends and others were dying after Katrina, mainly from stress and the almost insurmountable task of starting over. Soon my work project would be completed, and I too would have to seek another area in which I could apply my skills.

As usual, I accessed my problems, prayed about them and decided to tackle them patiently. I worked from the gut, and I was led to some answers, I am sure, through Divine intervention. Slowly over the next five years the mosaic pieces of my fragmented life fitted together to form a complete mental picture and led me to experience peace of mind.

My mother, in Memphis, following her relocation to the USA in 2006.

My parents together in Memphis in 2006.

Me, with my parents and my sister, in Las Vegas in 2006, fulfilling my 89 year old father's dream to see the city.

THE PAST FIVE YEARS

Repeatedly throughout my life, when I am at a crossroad, I have always taken the right direction. I am prepared to say that the solutions came as a result of Divine Intervention and the older I get the more convinced I am that it is so. One day during a regular 'town hall' meeting for Katrina's staff, I listened to a female speaker as she told us, that she represented a federal agency that relocated staff. This agency provided a choice of realtors to sell one's home, management services for rental property, assistance/ information on moving from one state to another. Assistance on storing one's furniture for up to two years and information on temporary housing until the move is finalized was shared. To mention just a few points that sounded like music to my ears. This information gave me hope. I wanted to move on, I wanted to sell my home, I needed to store my furniture until I was able to settle at my new address… and doing all this, as well as starting in a new job and relocating my parents seemed cataclysmic at the time. I was also 60 years old. However, I knew that I could not remain in New Orleans. I also knew that Mississippi was not my first choice to relocate and whatever happened I would continue with plans to relocate my parents. After listening to all the services that were available, I decided to work with this and any other agency that could help me to accomplish my goals.

There were some things in my favor. Prior to Katrina the house was recently painted and woodwork repaired. Only slight cosmetic changes inside were needed and a contractor from my church did this for a reasonable price. Some people were trying to return to the city and some were purchasing homes and relocating within the city. People were enquiring if our home was for sale even before the sign was posted. There was a job, similar to my present one, available in another state; this would mean that I would require only a brief orientation, if I was hired.

In December of 2005, I went to Kingston to be with my parents for their interview at the American Embassy. My purpose was to offer moral support. They could be denied and if that was the case, I needed to be there for them. Fortunately, the interview went well. In early March 2006 my home was put on the market and I was due to travel to Memphis to start a new job. It was a five hour road trip and about three hours into the trip, my realtor called informing me that a potential buyer had made an offer on the house. We were ecstatic!

Prior to moving to Memphis, my son was worried that I was doing too much at once. So together, we did a quiet tour, visiting my future home, locating the hospital, identify places to park, and driving around the city in order to acquaint me with my future home.

For the first two months in Memphis we lived in corporate housing. The job was going well, as predicted, orientation was brief, my colleagues were friendly and they made every effort to make transition from the 'Big Easy' smooth. My sister traveled to Jamaica to assist my parents with disposing of some possessions and to see and get a feel of potential buyers for their home. It was a very dynamic period, but we survived.

I tried, unsuccessfully, to find a house that I liked in Memphis, one that was near to the hospital. The realtor was very patient but somehow, I did not like any of her choices for me. Buying a house could not be done hastily and so I decided to continue living in rental property until I could be sure that I made the correct choice. I have to confess that I did not share this with the realtor and slyly I continued to tour Memphis with her and got her candid input on available property. Eventually I decided to find a larger apartment and did so at the end of May 2006. Some of our furniture was unloaded and this new apartment was prepared to accommodate my parents.

Now the travel date for my parents was set for June 2006 and I would travel with them. Their home was in the final stages of being sold and most of the contents were gone. We had occupied that home for forty six years and it felt strange locking the door for the last time. The neighbors were like family, they were very sad to see my parents leave, but silently they also feared for their safety and thought that my sister and I had made the right decision. They were also very impressed that I took time to travel with them. As far as I was concerned I wanted to travel with them in order to make their transition as stress free as possible.

The flight from Kingston to Miami went well. Our connection to Memphis was cancelled as the airport was shut down temporarily due to a horrific electric storm. Eventually we arrived in Memphis and with my parents in wheel chairs and two attendants loudly having their own conversation, as if we three were invisible, I could not find where I had parked my car. Finally, one attendant asked me…

'Miss, could you see outside when you parked your car?'

'No, I do not think so'…was my answer…

'Then you must have parked in the basement'.

He was correct. The car was found and we all piled in and we all traveled to the apartment to a new beginning for my parents.

The drive home went smoothly, ironically, our new home was located next to the Mississippi River. It was a very serene spot and my parents loved it! We went by the river frequently, just to walk, or sit in the car remembering old times and feeling relieved that the stress of being alone was over. My father would walk and count his paces, and estimate the distance that he walked each time. My mother would prefer to silently sit and 'people watch' and comment on familiar dress styles. Sometimes we would enjoy having picnic dinners while gazing at the river traffic and indulge in our fascination with the location.

I enjoyed living near to the river again and I was thankful to be away from the hurricane path. Just by chance, I found out that Memphis was situated on a seismic fault, and that was the deciding factor on future relocation.

Me, with my sister on another departure from the airport (Atlanta) in 2007.

JOLTED TO REALITY

I returned home one afternoon to overhear my husband telling my mother in a low, firm voice, that she did not make any decisions in this home, and that he was in charge. I was very perturbed and realized that both parents were very cautious while in his presence and that my father would not leave my mom alone with him. On this day, however, dad was not feeling well and he was resting in another room. They would not disclose, until after we were separated that my husband's behavior made them feel very uncomfortable. I was surprised, because this elderly couple was extremely kind and generous to us, especially early in our marriage. Also my husband's behavior was threatening, but naively, I never thought that he would subject my parents to his foul moods.

It was evident that I had to actively work on ending my marriage. I discovered that Tennessee was not a 'community property' state. I also realized that one of my colleagues at work was recently divorced and I decided to talk with her to get some advice on where to start. I had delayed facing this problem for too long; I finally made an appointment with a divorce lawyer.

Prior to my appointment, I mustered up enough courage to tell my husband that I wanted a divorce. I started by saying that we were both miserable and that we were quarreling frequently and it was clear that we were both unhappy. I still felt that I needed to be gentle. I still felt that I needed to make him an offer. I still did not want him to feel that I was deserting him. I am unable to explain why I had these feelings, why I felt guilty, but deep within me I did.

During my interview with the lawyer, she asked me,

'If things were that bad…why have you stayed this long?'

God knows I had no answer…except that mentally I was finally ready to admit that I had a big problem that I could finally talk about and resolve. She prepared my offer as I requested. However, my husband, after verbally agreeing to accept it, refused and got himself a lawyer and he just kept saying, when I asked if he was ready to discuss it…

'Not yet, I am waiting on my lawyer'.

So we waited.

The lease on the apartment was for a year, and I wanted to move at the end of this period. I missed living in a house and enjoying my own garden.

Finally, in early in May 2007 I realized that my husband refused my offer because he planned moving out of state with us. To me, this was the 'last straw' and I had hesitated long enough! The divorce papers were finally served. I did not want us to move on together to another state.

Work at the same time was going well, however on some issues, they were about a decade behind my previous administration, and it was frustrating to have to conform to methods that seemed unproductive. Also I wanted to do a lot more things with my life. I wanted to have a less restrictive work day. I looked at my friends at work and they were constantly in demand and very stressed. I regrouped and realized that I had worked since I was seventeen years old. I gave most of my life to raising my children. I had coped with my husband's erratic behavior, and now I was caring for my elderly parents. I now needed to pause and re-group mentally and choose how I was going to cope. I had not found a home in Memphis, I was really tired, of the daily work routine, thank God I had fairly good health…maybe I could relocate, and change my pace.

I shared these thoughts with my children and my parents and the search for a new home started. My first choice would be somewhere that was warm: a city that was not very big, one with public transportation, one that was conducive to older citizens, and was affordable, accessible, with a good international airport. A place with not too high a crime rate and finally one that was located in an area with not much pollution.

My first thoughts were Texas and Arizona. I thought of Texas, because I had a friend there, and of Arizona, because it was very warm and it sounded as if I could live there. Further research proved that these states were not good choices. My son told me about Athens… Georgia.

'You will like it'…he said. 'It is 'artsy', small, nice homes, the people also seem very friendly and eagerly give visitors information about the city; we could go and visit one weekend'.

I accepted his offer and I loved what I saw. We got a realtor who worked very well with us. My parents got all the information on the internet and loved what they saw. I finally bought a home in March 2007. It was arranged that my sister would 'house sit' until May when my parents would leave Memphis and I would retire the end of May and join them the first weekend in June. The separation from my husband and the move to Athens went well.

Thanks to good family support, the transition went well. It was good to be in a full house and to enjoy a garden again. It has been almost three years since the move and my retirement and I have not regretted it. Mentally I had to readjust my mind to the fact that I could sleep later each morning, and my schedule did not need to be crammed to the last minute, in fact I could be very flexible with my time and coping with the care of my parents. The greatest thing that I have gained from all these events is peace of mind. On one occasion I spoke with my ex-husband on the phone and when he started shouting, I was able to say,

'I will have to go now, as it is clear that you are not in a good mood', and I calmly disconnected the call.

Yes, my feathers are unruffled and my soul is at peace!

MY MOTHER AND DEMENTIA

I wanted to explain when I first noticed that my mother had dementia and I wanted to try to piece together how some events in her life may have enabled her to get to this stage. In my opinion, those facts are now irrelevant. The fact is that my mother has dementia and I am writing this from a caregiver's perspective. I used to find it very difficult to look at her small frame and not recall tearfully, the former days when she would garden for hours, or how she would arrange from green leaves, flowers and some driftwood, the most beautiful arrangements in our home. Looking further back, I remember how quickly she transformed some white fabric and gingham into a beautiful bedspread and curtains for our room. I remember how she would always have a meal for anyone who came by our home asking for money, and how she would invite some children over regularly on Sundays to have dinner with us.

In this world we never know how people with whom we come in contact can affect our later lives. Because of my mother's kind deeds, in her old age, many people protected her as they realized that her memory was failing.

Dementia was subtle, it certainly was undetected when I spoke with her on the phone. She would casually mention that her memory 'was not what it used to be', when we asked her to recall specific information. Also, because of her stubborn personality it was difficult to ascertain if she genuinely forgot, or simply refused to remember something. My father surprisingly adapted to the role as her caregiver very well; almost too well, my sister and I sometimes thought that he did not allow her to do more and that he seemed to be enabling her instead of allowing her to be more independent. It was easy for us to come to that decision and now I realize that we really were being unfair as we were not there all of the time , we only came to that conclusion from what we observed when we visited.

I watched other changes occur, as my mother would forget to bathe and to eat regularly, she misplaced things, she hid things so well that some were never found. Another change that occurred was that her facial expression was transformed into a blank vague stare, not appearing to focus on anything and not reflecting any emotion. She would sit with company but not initiate conversation and she would hardly move.

All this may sound very depressing and I hasten to add that it is only one aspect of her illness. My role as caregiver is difficult, especially at the end of the day when I am unable to interact with anyone else and to have a simple logical conversation. It is draining psychologically, but there are many good aspects of this role.

The main one is that although my mother has dementia, she has no physical illnesses. At ninety years old she is able to walk up and down stairs very well. She holds on to the banister and she may say that her knees are 'not what they used to be', but she tackles those stairs independently each day. She is still able to have her showers with minimal assistance. Her appetite is good. She still enjoys her occasional glass of Sherry with her dinner. With correct prompting and wearing her eye -glasses she will still play her favorite hymns on the keyboard. She is able to read without her glasses but when she is asked to play something, she will not budge without them. She still enjoys going to the cinema, to a good comedy and she loves going to musicals or choir recitals.

Now, there are times when, after a nap, she will look in my direction and say...

'Mr. Wilson' (as she would call my dad), 'what are we having for dinner today? I will just have a snack and you can fix something for yourself'.

Or she will look at me and ask seriously,

'Where did your father go today? I guess that we will have to wait until he gets here before we have dinner'.

Then I have to remind her that dad died. Sometimes, in response to that she will look at me as if she is hearing it for the first time, and sometimes she will say,

'I did not remember'.

On one occasion I took mom to the supermarket. I sat her down with a cup of coffee and a cupcake and I reassured her that I was just going to get two items and that I would return before she finished eating. After a very short time one of the employees recognized me and said that she was just about to page my dad to meet mom, because she told her that she was waiting on him. Then she realized what she had said and asked,

'Didn't you say that he had died?' As I nodded she also remembered that mom had dementia.

My mother has not forgotten how to love and there are times when she has lucid moments. She still recognizes her children and grandchildren and some names and faces of a few old friends. As a disciplinarian, she still says that children 'should be seen and not heard', a notion that young parents cannot relate to today. She never passes a young child without smiling or sometimes she reaches out to touch babies. This is sometimes not well received in today's stress filled world. She never receives a meal without saying 'God bless you' and without saying her grace. She never sleeps at night without reading from her Book of Psalms, and she is usually asleep within half an hour of getting into bed.

The best part of our day is at night when I tuck her in, if I remember to give her a kiss, she chuckles and says...

'That is the best thing that a mother could ever receive from her child' and she settles down to sleep, contented, like a young child at the end of a full day of play.

We feel blessed to be able to enjoy her company at this stage of our lives, and we cling to the few lucid moments when they occur and we are still fascinated by the mystery of the human brain as it is reflected in the behavioral changes of our beloved mother.

My mother celebrating her 91ˢᵗ birthday at a Red Hat luncheon in 2010.

THE RED HAT SOCIETY

I was visiting the New Orleans Museum of Art one Saturday and I noticed a small group of older women looking keenly at a portrait. They all wore red hats, I really did not notice if they were all dressed in purple, if they were I probably would have noticed. However, my first thought was that they represented a group that had survived some cardiac event. There was nothing more about this group that caught my attention at the time, and soon the episode passed. That was a long ago and I was busy working.

Some time afterwards, I heard about a group of women who wear red hats and purple dresses when they get together. The sole purpose of the group is to enjoy life and to have fun. The criterion for joining is that one has to be at least fifty years old. There are several of these groups in almost all the cities in the USA, It all started in California I learned, but now it is so appealing that it has attracted older women internationally.

I had spent most of my life working and raising my children and my husband. I had also spent many years living by the rules of a very controlling spouse and ignoring my quest to live life fully. My children urged me to go out more and to travel more and to interact more with groups and people outside of the church. My hobbies included writing, drawing, walking, singing and gardening…activities that I pursued alone.

'Mom, you need to interact with people more and to have fun', my daughter kept telling me.

She is outspoken, she does not hesitate to inform me if my colors do not coordinate, if my hair dye job failed, if my advice was not appropriate. My son, on the other hand waits for the right moment to say the plain truth… he thinks about it and then he informs me. Now this could be days after the event, but it would be at a time when I would be receptive to criticism. They are both protective and I love them both dearly.

Prior to marriage, I loved going to parties and having a good time. I was later told that with marriage came responsibilities and one did not need to 'behave like that'. Of course, my husband was nine years older than I was and he viewed life very differently. You can guess that we really never talked seriously about life and what we really believed in, prior to getting married. God knows I assumed that if we did not quarrel then we seemed compatible.

Well here, I, was, years later, trying to become a member of this fantastic group of women. I went to a luncheon in Athens, Georgia, and this group had no active queen (leader) because no one wanted the sole responsibility of coordinating events and so they still met regularly...to eat. They wore red hats and had fun, but they could not call themselves official members of the society.

'If you want to get into a group, they meet every first Wednesday at the Food Court in the mall', I was advised.

'All the Queens and some members from several groups meet there to share information on events and to interact with friends and to socialize over lunch. There you can see and decide for yourself which group you would like to join.'

Well I do not like hats, but I found a red baseball cap, and off to the mall I went one Wednesday morning. There were about twenty ladies there... they were laughing, telling jokes, recalling amusing events, and just enjoying themselves. One lady in the largest and fanciest hat was in a wheel chair and on oxygen...she was telling the best jokes. One talked of her pole dancing stint, and suddenly a cell phone ring sounded and she plucked her phone from her bosom...the site of her previous mastectomy and the now site for her phone. I was in awe....a new experience for me and just another day for these ladies. They were dressed in all shades of purple; they wore red shoes, some in sneakers that were artistically adorned with the red hat design. Some I noticed wore purple hats and red dresses...those were celebrating birthdays that month I was informed. I told them that I was new to Athens and that I would like to join the group. Almost immediately, I heard about what the different activities the groups were involved in, in order to enable me to make my decision. Some liked to dine out regularly, some did craft and made cards, some traveled and included trips to various places of interest, some did square dancing, and some did all of the above.

I now have the option to dine out and to be a part of tours to places that I would not have visited on my own. The beauty of this experience is that I am able to bring my mother with me. Although she has dementia, she is still able to enjoy a meal and good company and she likes music. The groups are welcoming towards her and it allows me to be able to get out of the house more and she gets to interact with more people…it has proven to be good for both of us.

These ladies are at various milestones of their lives, many have survived cancer, major surgeries, the death of a spouse, rough divorces, job lay offs, empty nest syndromes, returning children, career changes, to name a few. However, they remain focused on one fact…that life continues and one has to get together with the women and make the best of that day and have fun.

I have attended conventions that have been thoroughly heart warming. I remember the ninety year old mother of one of the sponsors 'bringing down the house' with her book of jokes…they were adult jokes and they were hilarious, and she said them with a stoic demeanor that added to the humor. We danced freely, easily, some better than others, but we danced.

The best part to me now, is dressing up for events. I do not like hats, but now I have a variety of sequined red and purple hats, berets and visors. Of course the aim is to work within one's budget and so swapping is common. I am also now discovering the art of simply spraying…with enamel…any plain straw hat and dressing it up with any decoration that is appropriate for that planned event. I still have a long way to go as my sister noted.

'Go to the 'girlie shops' and use your imagination…match pieces without breaking the bank…look at pieces that you would never dream of buying and try them on!'

That was advice that my daughter gave to my sister long ago and now it was my turn to be advised.

We love 'bling'. We wear 'diamonds' (rhinestones) on each finger, heavy sparkling red, or purple or rhinestone necklaces, broaches, earrings, bracelets and we wear them all in abundance, on our necks, arms, ears, waists, feet or blouses, wherever they can make a statement and we wear them with dignity and zest. We celebrate breakfast sometimes wearing our pajamas, we wear costumes at Halloween, Valentines Day, St. Patrick's day to name a few. We have wonderful pool parties in the summer, we host house parties and they are always good.

My best experience with this group was when I had a bereavement in my family. Those women came to my home and they sat with us. They came after the service and provided, served and cleared away afterwards, making sure that their Red Hat sister could cope. They were wonderful and they have a special place in my heart. Now I too give back to others during family events. I have learnt to smile, to laugh heartily, to meet each day as it comes, to email those who I have not seen or heard from for a while, to take time to enjoy what I see and whom I come in contact with, to easily reach out and share…time, ideas, company and love . It is truly a wonderful way to greet life.

There have been some sad moments for our group. Recently, one of our very active members died suddenly. Several of us attended her funeral, and we remembered the good times that we all shared, the most recent being Halloween, when her came dressed in a cat's costume. We all acknowledge that death is inevitable and felt that this woman lived every moment fully, finding time to enjoy her life. That was comforting.

The most recent wonderful celebration, for me, was at a convention in Myrtle Beach. I traveled with two other vibrant red hatters, and we had a wonderful experience. The weekend included shopping, touring nearby cities, dining and searching for restaurants that served oysters. One woman in our group enjoyed oysters, served in any form. We danced the nights away to Mo-Town oldies, enjoyed good wine and played board games. It was a whacky weekend, with a group of wonderful women, who knew how to have fun. The best 'eye-opener' came to me as I got to know one of our group members better. She is a very stately, sophisticated, soft-spoken person. She explained in detail how busy her schedule was. She hardly had time to ride 'as much as she would like'. I timidly asked what she rode, and chuckled as she said,

'A custom made three wheeled Harley Davidson.'

Me, dressed for an event at my first Red   *Me, after my divorce, at another Red*
Hat convention in 2008.   *Hat convention in 2009*

RECAPPING

I am not sure that there is a 'right time' to retire. Financial planners advise that it should be after one's mortgage debt is met. I know that for me, my body and soul decided that I needed to venture into another stage of my life. So retirement for me, in May 2007, has been good. The fact that I was able to retire and enter a new stage of my life has also been good. There were times when I never planned for retirement because I never dreamed that I would live that long. *My life's path has had many convolutions and many were unpredictable. Throughout the journey I have managed to meet each day, each obstacle, each surprise, each disappointment only with faith that God's assistance was always guaranteed, if I asked for it. It has not been easy; but to the reader I can only say that events happen and what one has to learn to do is to live through each event, learn from it and try to face the next one as it occurs. If I had given up after the disappointment of my first love/ relationship, I would never have left home for the United Kingdom, had my wonderful children, or become a nurse or started a new life in this country.*

I am glad that I chose to live in Athens and now I am busily involved with several groups:-

The Osher Lifelong Learning Institute (OLLI) and I am currently trying my utmost to learn to play the keyboard, and writing my memoirs, something that I have long wanted to do.

The Athens Area New Comers (AANC) and I have met some wonderful people, some have resided here for many years and some, like me, have been new comers. Through this group, I have managed to visit many local and nearby places of interest and of course enjoy the cuisine of local restaurants.

The Book Club (Women of Common Ground), an intriguingly diverse group of women. Here I learn to enjoy Merlot/ Cabernet, wonderful homemade food, and witty exchanges on life and sometimes of the books that we read.

The Red Hatters: this is another wonderfully diverse group of women who know how to pause and how to enjoy life. They have reminded me that it is OK to act crazy, to dress up, how to move forward, and I will never forget how they rallied behind my family when my father died.

I have joined classes offering Yoga and Tai Chi and again I can find time to relax my brain and meditate and maintain skeletal and muscle flexibility as I age.

I have been able to appreciate the Opera and the Arts again and to take advantage of free concerts and senior citizens discounts. I have met some wonderful and friendly people since arriving here. I have managed to be inviting and I have enjoyed being a hostess again. It has been wonderful.

Because of my divorce settlement, my projected retirement funds have been considerably reduced, but the peace of mind that I have gained through the dissolution of my marriage has enabled me to feel more contented with my life. I now realize that I am still able to live and that I am still able to afford to support my elderly mother and myself.

For years, I could have dissolved my marriage and I procrastinated. I feared that I would be unsuccessful and that I would not have the energy to tackle the task. I was afraid that maybe there would be violence. I also feared that financially, I would not be able to afford it. I hid from tackling this problem and consequently I exposed us to years of verbal and physical abuse from a husband and father who controlled the family with a psychological force. I allowed myself to be controlled; my children walked away long before I did.

The peace that I can enjoy now is through doing simple things, like sleeping late, going to bed and waking up in my own time and at my own pace. I can express my thoughts and opinions simply and calmly, without fear of confrontation. I can call and talk to my children and friends freely without worrying that my husband would hear and that he would use them as topics for more senseless arguments. I can receive my family freely when they visit and not have to be anxious that their presence would be fuel for future strife.

I am enjoying every moment of life and taking it all in my stride.

A BEAUTIFUL TRANSFORMATION

"She kissed him, she kissed him, ah huh, and I saw her."

"She put her arms around his neck and she said...bye honey".

The tiny demon's eyes beamed with unspoken childish pleasure as she uttered those words. The house was full of visitors who had come by to see my aunt who was visiting from America. I had heard so many beautiful stories about this woman and I was finally meeting her. She had been living in America for many years. Prior to that, she had visited England and Liberia. She had her fair share of tragedy, including losing her infant daughter a few years prior to this visit.

The little 'demon' was her younger and, now, only child, Terry Ann. She bore a strong resemblance to her mother and she, like most American children whom I met then, seemed to possess unlimited energy and consequently, was always involved in some mischief. I was eighteen years old, employed, dating a handsome, charismatic, romantic young man. I was going nowhere career-wise, but this supercharged child would not know that. I was an adult, and I was so embarrassed that this little child was responsible for my embarrassment and I was now furious.

Well, payback was not possible, I really could not whollop her, so eventually we became friends. Our age difference was twelve years. We met again when I was married and I then had my two children, who could have been ages ten and five. That would have put me at approximately 37 years old. This time I lived away from home with my husband and children. I was in an unhappy marriage. I was a full time working mother and wife. She was a beautiful, vivacious no nonsense young woman doing an undergrad degree on campus. It was a lovely visit, we were all older, but my time to enjoy this visit was limited, as I seemed to have difficulty juggling my hours between young children and a very demanding job and a husband. We did however find time to go to the theatre and to visit a botanical garden in the country.

I will now fast forward to 1997, 14 years after our last visit. This time it is my son's graduation. Her mother has been dead approximately three years. My cousin is now a beautiful wife of a friendly, lovable Russian, and mother of a vibrant adorable six-year-old boy.

This meeting had me smiling silently; there were numerous stories of the challenges of motherhood from her. Some included a small child (her son) shouting 'child abuse' in the restaurant, while his young parents attempted to discipline him. Alternatively, the same small child threw his shoe out of the moving family car on the interstate, probably to get their undivided attention. I also remember both parents trying to coax this 'angel' out of his winter woolies (his thick winter coat), during an abnormally sunny May graduation venue in New Hampshire. He kept them on, I would like to add for the record.

This Thanksgiving we all got together for a small reunion. The 'little angel' is now a handsome 19-year-old freshman on campus in New York, a very calm, mature, well focused young adult. His mother is beautiful. She is the image of my aunt, her mother. She has the kindest heart, and a wonderfully, outreaching personality. She is also a very generous person and a wonderful mother and wife.

Time changes us all. We had a wonderful time. We met yet more family, second cousins and their children. We, the older ones were able to tell some of the cousins stories of their grandparents that they had never heard before. We watched familiar family traits become evident in the younger members and could almost instantly liken them to similar traits in a parent. We smiled and afterwards noted with glee that genes could not be denied…some of the childhood rascalities were again evident in their children. It was a wonderful reunion. That night I retired with a satisfied smile. Small family events are now satisfying pleasures that add to the contentment of my soul.

AT FULL BLOOM

On completion of this chapter, I will be able to cross another item from my 'bucket list'. For the readers who do not know what that means, it is a list of things to do in ones lifetime. The idea was the theme of a comedy that was filmed, starring Jack Nicholson and Morgan Freeman. Other items on my Bucket List include writing and publishing some poetry and inspirational thoughts and learning to ride a horse. I have no idea how I will accomplish the latter, but I will certainly try.

I continue to enjoy life in Athens. Caring for my mother has been difficult. The hardest part of that role, to me, is at the end of the day. That is when I like to sit quietly, sometimes with a small glass of sherry and reminisce. I like to talk about what I did in the garden, or what happened that day, or some recent event that was good or about the old relatives or the children. Dementia has robbed me of sharing more memories with my mother. Sometimes I even doubt if she does not remember, or if she is simply being stubborn and refusing to recall another family story. I will never know. On the other hand, having seen and cared for many people with dementia, many are in Nursing Homes to make it easier on their families. Many simply wander away from home, or get very hostile and exhibit a complete character change with this diagnosis. I am still able to cope with Mom at home. I am also able to share this role with my sister and we both get our psychological breaks to maintain our sanity. In other words, compared to others with dementia, it could be a lot worse for us.

I continue to enjoy my family and friends and am never bored with my new role. Life happens, and it is to be lived to the fullest and each moment is to be enjoyed.

To my children I say, there are many strong personalities in the family. The ones that I remember are my paternal grandparents. My grandfather was a landowner and a sort of an entrepreneur. My grandmother was a quiet, practical, no-nonsense, loving, single mother, who survived typhoid fever. My maternal grandparents: my grandfather was a career law enforcement officer and my grandmother was a fiercely opinionated single mother.

In our family there were many elderly aunts, many of whom were teachers and nurses. One even formed her own school. Two of my aunts traveled to Africa in the early 1920's and 1930's, one as a missionary. The family has also produced two judges, many lawyers, two doctors and an Olympian. There are also World War II and Korean War Veterans in the family. All of this occurred through receiving a sound education and grasping the opportunity to travel. Currently, several young cousins continue working as lawyers, accountants, nurses, teachers, policy makers, writers, preachers and university professors. Many of them have settled in countries miles from the tiny island of Jamaica.

Each day brings new challenges to us all, and we continue to move forward with determination, a family trait. If one of the obstacles in our life's path appears as a high wall, we will try to find a way to climb over it, or we will go around it. Sometimes, we even have to grab the appropriate tools and dig a tunnel under it. But one thing is sure, in time, and with God's grace, we do overcome.

MY CHILDREN

I write this with love and admiration. You are both wonderful individuals and, like the average mother, I am biased, but I am proud of you both. You both persevered through school and colleges with set goals and maintained focus on your goals. You both seemed to understand, very early, that frequent shopping days, access to numerous credit cards, flashy cars, early car ownership while attending high school, numerous parties and flashy designer clothes were not a priority on our list.

I know that you both must have had a hard time coping with all the changes that we had to make as a family with relocating and adopting a new culture very early in your lives. Throughout all this God has been gracious, and we can look back, not with astonishment and surprise at achievements, but with positive recognition that with God's help, our paths were guided, and on many occasions, we were carried by Him for the difficult sections of our journey. The journey will continue as long as there is life. There are things that we each can change, and some that we cannot change. I pray that you both will have the wisdom to walk away from what you cannot change and use your energy working with others towards making a positive difference.

Before any of this can be accomplished, remember that you both have to continue to be comfortable with who you are. Thanks for your honesty. Thank you for accommodating me in your homes and thanks for involving me in your adult lives. The most difficult part of my being a mother to adult children is being able to step back, recognize that my opinion is politely heard, but not taken, and learning to cope with that reality.

Promise me that you both will never waste time clinging to trying to get even with whom may have done you wrong. Always continue to cultivate a forgiving heart and spirit. Always treat others as you would like to be treated. Strong personal growth and development will be impeded by negativity. God is always in control and eventually we will all be accountable to Him for our decisions in this life. Our mission on earth is one of love.